COIN COLLECTING

Learn How to Collect Rare and Valuable Coins

(The Official Guide to Coin Collecting and Stamp Collecting)

Walter Yanez

Published By Walter Yanez

Walter Yanez

All Rights Reserved

Coin Collecting: Learn How to Collect Rare and Valuable Coins (The Official Guide to Coin Collecting and Stamp Collecting)

ISBN 978-1-77485-408-2

All rights reserved. No part of this guide may be reproduced in any form without permission in writing from the publisher except in the case of brief quotations embodied in critical articles or reviews.

Legal & Disclaimer

The information contained in this book is not designed to replace or take the place of any form of medicine or professional medical advice. The information in this book has been provided for educational and entertainment purposes only.

The information contained in this book has been compiled from sources deemed reliable, and it is accurate to the best of the Author's knowledge; however, the Author cannot guarantee its accuracy and validity and cannot be held liable for any errors or omissions. Changes are periodically made to this book. You must consult your doctor or get professional medical advice before using any of the suggested remedies, techniques, or information in this book.

Upon using the information contained in this book, you agree to hold harmless the Author from and against any damages, costs, and expenses, including any legal fees potentially resulting from the application of any of the information provided by this guide. This disclaimer applies to any damages or injury caused by the use and application, whether directly or indirectly, of any advice or information presented, whether for breach of contract, tort, negligence, personal injury, criminal intent, or under any other cause of action.

You agree to accept all risks of using the information presented inside this book. You need to consult a professional medical practitioner in order to ensure you are both able and healthy enough to participate in this program.

TABLE OF CONTENTS

INTRODUCTION 1

CHAPTER 1: WHAT EXACTLY IS NUMISMATICS? 4

CHAPTER 2: WHAT YOU SHOULD TO LOOK FOR IN A COIN 22

CHAPTER 3: OLD COINS AS COLLECTIONS 27

CHAPTER 4: THE TYPES AND SPECIALTIES OF COIN COLLECTORS 34

CHAPTER 5: COIN COLLECTING OFFERS A GLIMPSE INTO THE PAST 41

CHAPTER 6: PRESERVING, AND PROTEGATING YOUR COLLECTION 46

CHAPTER 7: MAKING MONEY 65

CHAPTER 8: HOW TO PURCHASE COINS 86

CHAPTER 9: GRADING SERVICES 97

CHAPTER 10: GOLD COIN COLLECTING 102

CHAPTER 11: THE WAY TO COLLECT COINS LIKE A PRO . 106

CHAPTER 12: THE FUNDAMENTALS OF COIN COLLECTING 128

CHAPTER 13: SPECIAL COIN SETS 143

CHAPTER 14: FINDING RARE AND COLLECTIBLE COINS .. 169

CHAPTER 15: SELLING YOUR COIN COLLECTION 174

CONCLUSION 182

Introduction

It's never either too late or too late to enjoy a hobby. Some individuals enjoy hobbies for enjoyment but others look at the bigger scope, and are looking to generate revenue. Things that seem small now could be worth it or useful later on.

Some excellent examples include sports cards, stamps, toys and cards. Many people have made money through the sale of their collectibles auction sites such as eBay. Another pastime that could be profitable is collecting coins.

It's as easy as choosing the kind of collection you want. Coins are produced annually and some are released several years later, therefore making sure you are focusing on a particular date and time is crucial.

Doing some research with online resources or reference books can help with collecting coins. There is a lot of information available about coins that are worth keeping.

The best sources for information are publications on coins such as Coin World or Coinage Magazine. A local coin shop could further expand the search for antique coins outside the state or city of the collector.

A coin club can create a collector's community. A few members may wish to sell a particular coin to exchange it for another or another, and so on.

The coins that are not used are usually more valuable than coins that are operational, because earlier coins were made using 100% silver or gold. Given that market for coins made of silver has increased and they were difficult to produce today, they are made with 60% and 40 percent copper.

When you've finished the collection The coins should be placed in a sturdy case or folder. This will keep them neat and easy to carry around and display.

Coins can get cleaned through soaking in one of these solutions like rubbing alcohol, vinegar or lemon juice and ammonia, which will eliminate any dirt or encrustation that was present on the coin at the time it was first minted. Then, they need to be dried in the air or wiped dry using the help of a soft cloth. Rubbing or polishing the coins isn't recommended as it causes scratches and will decrease the value on the market for the coin.

Chapter 1: What exactly is Numismatics?

The most commonly used definition of numismatics refers to the systematic study and collection of coins. So numismatics, although in a limited sense, is now known as coin collection. However, the term can be applied to the collection of different objects used for money, like tokens, paper money, and medals, such as stocks certificates, checks and other objects that represent both financial assets as well as liabilities. However, it is a fact that numismatics is commonly equated with coin collecting. Over the years this pastime, once described as "the sport of the monarchs" due to its renowned founders has now become an extremely well-known and renowned.

The oldest of hobbies around the globe.

The people who study the science of numismatics as well individuals who actively collect coins, are known as "numismatists." They generally have an passion for Ancient Greek or Roman coins as well as medieval or hammered coins, and modern-day minted coins.

Although numismatic objects such as those listed above are of primary commercial and economic value but they also hold a significant historical and artistic merits. Coins are also important in archeology because they are a reflection of the particularity of the people or the time in which they were created. Numismatics is a reflection of the social, economic cultural, political and artistic styles that were prevalent in the period. If a large demand is present for their collection their intrinsic numismatic value could increase over their value in the current.

Since numismatics covers a vast selection in materials it provides a an endless and a vast array of possibilities, not just to have fun as a hobby and as a source of source of inspiration to explore and learn.

A.

A Brief Introduction to Coins and Coin Collecting

The term "numismatics," or coin collecting as it's commonly known, originates out of the Greek word "nomisma," which means legal currency, or coin. While we today use notes on paper, checks, and more frequently plastic cards, early societies used coins to make everyday purchases. The first coins that are known to have been made came of Lydia which is located in Asia Minor which today is part of Turkey however was under Greek influence back then. They are dated to over 2,600 years in the past. These first coins were created from gold and

silver alloy. The

Lydians were attracted to business, and could build an economic society that was able to make advances in commerce and trade. Coins from this time period show the evolution of design of coins throughout the history.

At the time the most popular method of payment was small pieces of silver and gold ingots. Since there was no standardization at the time and there were a lot of dishonest merchants, every transaction that involved the payment of silver and gold required a careful weighting of the item. Coins were invented around 650 B.C. and were produced using standard weights of silver and gold. The government stamped them with a guarantee of its worth. The following century saw the growth of the coin as the primary means of trade.

It is believed that the interest in collecting coins started when that first piece of coin created. Because banks were not in existence during that time, collecting them appeared to be a sensible method of storing the coins. They were not just for their intrinsic value, but also because of their rarity. These coins are now a family heirlooms, passing from one generation to next.

There are those who believe that genuine coin collecting started in the early Middle Ages when many European monarchs actually searched for and collected rare coins that were used as tenders in ancient societies. One of the interesting things they discovered was that each coin was unique because of the way of making them. Coins were struck manually at the time, and it was in the 1500's that coins were produced by machines. Since those European monarchs began collecting coins, this pastime is often called"the "Hobby that Kings."

Coin collecting was popular in the Renaissance era and entrepreneurial people started creating several high-quality forgeries. These forgeries are given an enviable price due to their value, quality, and historical value.

Ancient Roman Coin

The United States, the first coins were made from copper, and were struck by the Philadelphia Mint starting in 1793 in the context of the Coinage Act. The production at the time was done manually with coins being struck in one piece at a. The government later opened more US mints to identify coins that were struck at each branch; a system of mint marks was created on March 3rd 1835. Rules were enacted to distinguish coins with stamps at every branch. They were designed to ensure the an oversight of all coins and ensure that production of coins was common to everyone.

Modern numismatics is an analysis of the mid-1700s century to the 21st century's coins. In this time when coins first began to be struck with machines. While ancient coins drew attention from historians, scholars, and archeologists because of their archeological and historical significance Modern numismatics meets the demands of collectors and amateur collectors. It is focused on the evaluation of the coin's importance, based upon their manufacturing and usage. Other topics that are of importance in modern numismatics are coins of various varieties, errors made by mints,

The result of wear and tear on dies as well as the result of progressive die wear, mint markings and figures.

A group of collectors in 1858 small group of collectors established an organization called the American Numismatic Society (ANS) as an international non-profit organisation which promotes the preservation and study of coins as well as other numismatic objects like papers and medals. The most sought-after types of coins by collectors of the present are those with historical significance, are the appearance of mint mistakes, as well as limited issues or commemorative coinage. As a result an important talents that a coin collector has is the ability to evaluate coins with precision.

B.

How do coins get made? The Minting Process

If you're new at collecting coins, understanding the way in which coins are created can assist you in understanding the various types of coins. It can help you understand the reason why some types are referred to as non-circulated coins, while other types are known as resistant coins.

1.

Ancient Coins

In the early days artisans were responsible for creating everything from kitchen appliances to agricultural tools. Their responsibilities included the creation of coins. They employed simple tools, and the result was based on their expertise. It is worth noting that the quality of coins struck differs, from that of "widow's mite" of Palestine to the stunning silver coins from Greek Sicily.

Widow's Mite Coins

The most basic tools that craftsmen used included an oven to heat blanks, or "flans" as well as tongs, anvils that were set on a bench or table and a pair dies that were used for imprinting the design onto the flan. Iron or hard bronze was used to create dies. The wear of bronze was faster, however it was much easy to engrave and was not rusty. For their biggest coins they used bronze. Greeks employed iron dies, where the traces of rust can be seen. The artists placed the obverse die on an anvil and to create the impression, it was struck on the reverse.

2.

Modern US Coins

The modern-day coinage in the US began within the public sector. Private firms produced planchets, coinage blanks, and other supplies that which the US Mint purchased. The US Congress approved the Coinage Act that created the United States Mint in 1792 as a part of the US Department of Treasury. Prior to that, a variety of currency types, including colonial and foreign, were utilized. The new law mandated the establishment of a national mint

is located in Philadelphia located in Philadelphia, which was the capital city at the at the time. It is located in Philadelphia, which was the capital at that time. US Mint is in charge of producing, selling and securing the nation's currency and other assets. The institution produces between 14 to 28 billion of circulating coins . In the year 2004, between 65 and 80 million coins are produced each day. Only coins produced from the US mint are recognized to be US legally valid tender.

American Coins

All the materials that are used in making US coins are purchased from commercial producers. It is the US Mint gets one-cent coin blanks that are already produced, but creates the blanks for five-cent coins as well as the cupsronickel-clad coins made from strips of.

The process of manufacturing for every denomination is identical. However dimes, quarters half dollars , and dollars are made through a procedure known as "

Reeding" that is a way to mark these coins with tiny ridges. These ridges prevent cutting off or cutting the precious metal contained in silver and gold coins. Although it may not be important today, but it is practiced in respect to the long-standing practice that goes back to the colonial times. It's also intended to help visually impaired people identify coins.

It is required by law of the present that all coins in circulation bear the following insignia: "Liberty," "In God We Trust," United States of America," and "E Pluribus Unium," with each coin's denomination and the year of its issue. Its phrase "In God We Trust" is used continuously in the 1 cent coin from 1909 and on the ten cent currency since. Since the 1st of July, 1908 all silver coins, gold dollars, quarter-dollar coins, and quarter coins were also able to carry this motto.

3.

The Minting Process (Source: http://www.usmint.gov/)

Coins are made of metal. In order to make coins, several intricate steps are required beginning with the preparation of the raw materials to the final coin's sculpting. These are the streamlined steps of the coin minting process.

Step 1. Blanking

The U.S. Mint buys strips of steel that measure 1500 feet and 13,200 inches in width for the production of the nickel, dime quarter half-dollar, dollar and nickel. The strips are then rolled into coils. Each coil goes through an abrasive press that produces round discs known as blanks. The remainder strip, also known as webbing, is cut and reused. (To make the cent stamp, the Mint purchases blanks to stamp after providing fabricators with zinc and copper.)

Blanks are planchets which do not have passed through all the necessary processes before they are turned into coins. A planchet is a piece of paper that has gone through all of the steps required and is ready to be struck. The blanks are typically bigger than the final coins and are rough edges known as burrs. These are then removed as the next steps.

2. Annealing Drying and washing

They are heated in an annealing furnace , which helps soften the material. They are then run through a dryer and washer.

The final rolling and process of blanking causes the blanks to become hard. They are heated to the control of temperatures that range from 1400 to 1400°F. The process of annealing reduces the crystal structure, making it easier to work on. Since this leads to lower strike pressure, the lifespan of the dies used for coining is increased.

The process of annealing can cause discoloration of the blanks. To get rid of these the blanks are then tumbled against one another before being put through a chemical bath. After that, they are dried with the help of forced hot air . If necessary the blanks are taken to the mill that is upsetting them.

Step 3. Ridding

After upsetting, the blanks are screened over "riddles" to identify those that are not correct in shape or size.

Step 4: Disrupting

The good blanks are put into an upsetting process. This creates a rim on the edges.

The upsetting mill consists of a wheel with a groove along its edge that fits into a curved piece which has its own groove. The raised rim that is created during the process is shaped and sizes the blank to improve flow through the press. It also will harden the edge to prevent the leakage of the metal in between the die's obverse and collar.

Step 5 5. Striking

After that, the blanks go to the press for coining. They are then stamped by hand with their designs, inscriptions and designs that ensure they are genuine United States coins.

Step 6 Step 6: Inspecting

Press operators with magnifying glasses spot-check every batch of freshly struck coins.

Step 7 Step 7: Bagging and counting

Finally, the coins are weighed using an automated counting machine, and are placed into large bags. The bags are sealed and loaded onto pallets and stored in vaults. New coins are delivered via truck into Federal Reserve Banks. Then the coins are sent to the local bank!

4.

Coin Distribution

The US Mint continually modifies its methods for estimating demand for coins. This ensures that there is a smooth and efficient circulation of US coins. This is to ensure that the US Mint employs economic indicators as well as historical trends in seasonal patterns to manage production and delivery schedules. This is also used to calculate numbers regarding the production as well as distribution and circulation of the coins. Forecasting isn't accurate, so production should take into account any possible deviation. Usually, armored tractor-trailer vehicles are used to transport coins.

United States Mint, Philadelphia, PA.

Chapter 2: What You Should to look for in a coin

Coin collecting is a great activity to start. The excitement of looking to find old-fashioned coins sufficient for many people to continue doing it. Some people, however think of the collecting of coins as an investment decision, one they could make money by.

Many coin collectors will search for a specific kind of coin. They will enhance their collection and appealing to buyers. Some are collecting coins to satisfy sentimental value and paying greater at the authenticity of the coin.

Series collectors are people who want to collect every date on each occasion the coin was created. They aim to collect one that marks every change in design and year. Type collectors are people who are seeking to own every coin that has modifications.

The coin collectors of the past were who are looking for coins from the years 650 BC to around 450 AD. The time when coins were invented and varieties of bronze and goldm silver of the same. This also marks the time in which Roman Emperors were the ruling class and the majority are based on famous Roman cities, Roman emperors and gods.

Token collectors try to discover different kinds of tokens used to exchange cash in the event of no coins. These tokens were used as local currency , even though the government had not allowed the use of these tokens.

Coins are also assessed. The grading of a coin is based on its conditionand its value will depend heavily on the grade. It is crucial for any coin collector to know how to grade a coin in order to make sure he doesn't get scammed by people who are looking to earn a quick buck.

Uncirculated coins are those that do not have any wear or tear, or, to use a more commonly used term, they are in mint state. Mint state (MS) grade is determined on contact marks hairlines, luster, and general attraction. Coins can be graded as ranging between MS-60 (dull luster) to an MS-70 perfect. Although MS-70 is often considered to be unattainable an MS-65 grade and higher is likely to increase the value of a coin.

Coins that are circulated have more flexibility. they do not take into account how much dirt or scratches a particular coin has been exposed to over the years. Coins that have been circulated are likely to vary. AU (about non-circulated) and (about uncirculated), EF (extremely exquisitely) (extremely fine), very fine, VF (very extremely fine) F (fine) (fine), very fine, VG (very excellent) G (good) and AG (around decent) F-2 (fair) and P (poor) are used to determine what a coin's worth.

These grades are determined by the luster of a coin that has been circulated and visible wear, its style aspects, and the presence of characters and letters.

Contrary to uncirculated coins' grades they do not significantly diminish the value of a coin. This is perfect for people who want to complete their collection and don't want to worry about mint condition.

The price of a coin will to be influenced by the coin's demand and supply. Incredibly low supply and massive demand are likely to increase the price of a coin higher. However, the huge supply of coins will reduce the value of a coin.

Demand is usually created through coin dealers who look at the people looking to buy coins and the amount of people who sell the coins. If a coin ends up being difficult to locate the dealers will tend typically raise the cost more expensive so that it will increase the number of people willing to purchase additional copies of the coin.

The process of grading and pricing coins usually requires a significant amount of knowledge and experience to master. While there are many guidelines and rules to look for when it comes to grading coins professionals are the only ones who are the final word about what the value of a coin. It is not a bad idea to know the process of grading and the reason why your coin was assessed in a different way than what you've observed.

Coin collecting isn't just an investment in financial wealth but rather fun and enjoyable. While the main goal of a coin-collector is to complete a set, figuring out what you are looking for within a particular coin vital to ensure that no one else will benefit from your need to complete a particular set.

Chapter 3: Old Coins as Collections

The process of collecting coins is great enjoyable! It's a great hobby as well as a source of income for many. One kind of coin you may want to think about collecting are ancient coins. A lot of collectors avoid buying antique coins for collection simply because they're costly. The most important thing is the distinctiveness of these coins as well as the benefits they offer collectors.

Here are some suggestions to keep in mind when purchasing ancient coins:

1. Conduct a study on ancient coins. It is vital that a collector be aware of which coins are considered as ancient. It is not necessary for the collector to visit libraries since a variety of websites on the Internet will provide all the information required to be informed about old coins.

2. There are a variety of coins from the past available to collectors. Collectors

have the option of choosing from a variety of eras and civilisations. You can choose from Chinese civilization or an old Rome, Greek, Persian and so on. It is best for collectors to concentrate on a particular type of group or era of coins when collecting them.

3. Once a choice is established, a collector may decide to invest in the purchase of the coins. For starters, choose coins that are the least expensive, set the price at $20. When the collection is growing and the collection grows, the person may be tempted to buy higher-end coins.

4. A collector may also consider seeking out ancient coins through auction houses, or at online auctions where old coins are offered. Beware of fraud regardless of which site you use, and exercise extra care when purchasing coins from auctions online.

5. It is recommended that the collector create an inventory of all the older coins he wants to acquire. They can be listed

according to the order in which he would like them. preference. This will make the hunt for old coins more straightforward. The first thing on the list must be the amount the buyer is willing to pay for a particular type of coin. This list will prove useful regardless of whether it is on the internet and at an auction and will help him manage the budget without difficulty.

6. It is crucial to have a different holder for the collection of coins he has accumulated over time as well as other collections. Separate holders aid the collector in organizing and keep his treasures. Coins from the past are typically more costly than other coins of collectibility, therefore it is crucial for collectors to be aware of how to take care of their coins.

Old coins shouldn't scare coin collectors. They're an enjoyable way to experience the joy that is collecting coin. They are not just entertainment, but they also act as a resource of knowledge for a lot of coin collectors.

Coin Collecting Album

For any numismatist or coins collectors, finding a suitable spot to store their precious valuable coins can be the important thing to do because keeping their valuable coins in a secure and safe location will ensure that the authenticity and value of their coins are maintained...

There are numerous kinds of storage space that can assist you in keeping and displaying your coins. You can utilize holders, folders and plastic tubes or even the album, however among these storage options the coin collection albums are the best method to display your coins.

If you'd like to learn more about the reasons behind albums there are quite a couple of advantages of albums. You can also analyze the concept based on them:

1. Two-way image viewing

Coin collecting albums are a great way to ensure you can feel more content seeing your collection because albums let you view both sides of your coin. You don't need to take away your coins each time you wish to view the other side.

Thus, albums provide the best possible of both.

2. Greater defense against instant wear

Another benefit of albums over folders and other forms of storage options is that they offer the coins more protection from damaging elements that can speed up the degradation in the condition of coins.

Albums are typically distinguished through the usage of plastics to protect against environmental and scratch marks.

3. A good coin holder

Albums come with pockets for coins storage. The benefit of using an album can be that "dilapidated" coins, or extremely damaged coins are more secure.

Coins that have been tossed out, put in folders, suffer from the unsettling tendency to drop out and again. In coin collection albums, they remain in place.

4. Variation in price

Albums that are utilized in collection of coins typically cost from $20 to $40. While they may be costly, they offer more storage space for your most sought-after precious treasures. The cost of an album can be a wonderful alternative to other kinds of storage.

5. Information center

These albums are excellent "information centers" in the sense that collecting is concerned because they are the majority of albums that allow you to put in the essential details about your collection. The album also comes with an interior cover that gives the space to store the storage of your "mintage models."

The process of collecting coins is easier and enjoyable thanks to these albums. This makes your treasures last longer and thus, creating more value for them.

Thus, coin-collecting albums are the most effective "keepers" of your valuable coins.

Chapter 4: The Types and Specialties of Coin Collectors

As a coin-collector What would you say about your self? This field is divided into various categories. Here's the way you can be a part of one:

The most frequent collectors or those who just collect at a moment's notice

You'll know you're an individual belonging to this group If:

Whatever your age regardless of your age, you have coins to show off.

You randomly gathered without a strategy.

You shouldn't be spending a lot of cash on care for coins or other purchases.

You can find old coins or coins that have errors as well as coins that are no longer in circulation.

A second-level collector or a curious one

If one of the following applies to you, then you could belong to this category:

You are a collector because you love your hobby more than simply because someone gifted you a collection kit as a present.

You spend money building up your collection by buying new coins.

It is common to visit automobile dealerships to see what new products they provide.

You'll spend some time on the internet searching for coins on websites like eBay.

You don't have a precise purpose for your collection.

You'd like to know more about collecting coins and have thought about doing so in the field like using a notepad or level.

The most important collector in the field

If one of the following applies to you, then you could be classified as:

You dedicate a substantial amount of time engaged in this noble leisure activity

You're a collector who likes diversification, and is always looking for new places to buy coins from. In the end you'd like to complete the collection.

It's best to finish the series, because there are a variety of incomplete series

If you don't have sufficient resources, then you can decide what you have, and complete the sequence.

If you're an avid collector of coins or other kind of collector It isn't necessary to classify yourself. But, for reasons of self-promotion some people prefer to label themselves professional, amateur or novices. Professionals in all fields is generally someone who earns money by doing what they love. In terms of skill or passion an amateur could be as talented as an expert, but they don't earn money from their passion. If you're interested in learning more about the various kinds of collectors who collect coins, utilize search engines like Yahoo and Google to gain more knowledge about the topic. It is certain that this article has helped in getting a better knowledge of the class that you are currently a part of. The majority of people start with the beginner level and progress through the third and second levels. Some are, however proceed straight to the professional level, for instance those who want to start a business to earn cash by opening an online store selling coins.

A Few Tips To Start In Collecting American Coins

Coin collecting is a great activity that anyone from any walks of life and any age can enjoy If they're willing to put in the effort and sometimes some money to put into.

The precious metal gold is a precious metal.

The federal government of the United States of America issues gold coins to be used in general circulation from 1838 and. In the beginning, Liberty head served as a design imprint up to 1907. This design later revised to incorporate the popular Indian head bust as well as the St. Gaudens motif, and the design remained in production until 1933. Then, the notorious Great Depression began, necessitating cuts in all areas in American life. This led to the fact that the gold coins were returned to the mint, which made these coins extremely scarce and, like other precious items they are a collector's delight. This famous double eagle was the most sought-after item in this particular category. This is a coin worth $20 that was introduced just after the famed Californian gold rush of the 1800s. The coin was not permitted to circulate until the 1930s and, at the time it went to auction off in 2002, it sold for $8 million. But gold coins aren't easy to come across and that's the reason why only a few individuals collect them.

Defects

The coins that are damaged or were not printed correctly by the mint well-liked by collectors. If you happen to come across coins that have been printed incorrectly or have spelling errors, or are adorned with a design that is not appropriate be aware that you might be lucky to possess them. In auctions, they could be sold for as much as 10,000 dollars.

Apart from the two categories mentioned above, limited-edition coins are popular for collectors. Be aware that your collection will appeal more by focusing on one particular category instead of seeking to become a master of all trades. Certain collectors collect only pennies, whereas others are interested in nickels and dimes... A different alternative is to not pay attention to coin and concentrate on a specific period of time. For instance, you may be looking to collect items from during The Great Depression. The thing to be aware of is that you should accumulate the category you are interested in until you have it all. Keep collecting 1930s pennies until you've collected enough for each year. This is the most basic category that we discussed earlier. As you get more knowledge in the game, you'll naturally set higher standards for yourself.

It can be a hassle for collectors who are new with the hobby since it could take months, or even years to finish a collection. Some, on the other hand are thrilled. The feeling of satisfaction which comes from finishing the series is definitely worth the long wait.

Chapter 5: Coin Collecting Offers A glimpse into the Past

The correct term for collecting coins is the term numismatics. Whatever you decide to refer to it it is a cherished hobby that has endured for hundreds, or thousands of years.

Everyone has probably collected one or two coins due to a reason or another. Perhaps you simply loved the look of it or the date that had a personal significance for you. Have you ever took the quarters of every state and attempted to collect an entire collection?

Coins provide a wealth of information about the past of a civilization or country. Due to this, they hold historical significance and also their value as a currency. Numerous coins are struck in the image of an emperor, king queen or president.

The majority of coin collectors who are amateurs begin with coins that originate from their country because they are easily accessible.

In the near future, the fascination could grow more focused, for example, keeping only one particular type of coin. Commemorative coins are attractive for collectors.

Amateur coin collectors should be wary of fake coins that regularly appear on the market. In the absence of an expert on the subject, it's difficult to distinguish fake coins which are sold as genuine.

If the item you are looking for is expensive, it is essential to get the coin authenticated through an authentication service for coins. The condition of the coin is a factor to its worth, so it is essential to know the quality of the coin.

If you are serious about collecting coins, it is essential to buy the right containers to store your coins. If your coins are stored in a container they might get scratched. The value of the coins will decrease. Coin cases, trays, or CDs are available to store your coins.

Unexpectedly, washing coins may actually decrease the value of the value of a collection. Collectors want to see the coins in their original condition. Minerals in tap water may cause damage to coins, and hard fabrics can scratch the surface of the coin.

An Introduction to Rare Coins

Coins that are unusual are more valuable than the common coin inside your pockets. Rare coins are typically caused by an error, but sometimes the coins are circulated before the mistake is discovered.

The error isn't obvious to the untrained eye the coins could remain in circulation for a long time before falling in the laps of a collector. What a thrill to the collector of coins who comes across an unusual discovery!

Have you ever heard that certain coins that are in circulation are worth over $2,000? It's a bit disheartening to know that you might have handed this precious coin to someone else as exchange for one dollar.

Rare coins with printing Errors.

The printing errors of mistakes are the source for many of the rare coins still in circulation. One instance is a nickel issued in 1964. Since the plate was regularly cleaned, some of the letters had been scratched off. Collectors noticed this and immediately began to reserve every one they could locate.

Another error resulted in an unlucky coin being called"the Atheist Cent. A metal blob obscured the part of an inscription that reads "In God We Depend". The coin instead said "In God".

When the mark is not perfect, it prompts coin collectors to use their sharp eyes to identify these errors. The Philadelphia first began to use an official mint mark in the year 1980, but by 1982, some coins were issued without mint marks. They were extremely valuable for collectors.

Sometimes, the die fails to fire and stamps the coin twice. This can be a great experience for serious collectors.

Coins printed using the wrong Metals.

Over time, many precious metals were used to create specific American coins. Sometimes, the incorrect metal was employed, and the mistake was only discovered when the coins were in circulation.

As you can see, becoming an expert coin collector demands having a keen eye and a keen eye for the finer details. Many people don't look at the coin with such attention. Additionally, a thorough understanding is required if you're likely to spot rare coins once they are found in your possession.

Chapter 6: Preserving, and Protegating Your Collection

It's not worth it to collect coins if you'll throw them in the trash and display them nakedly in your cabinet or perhaps not even look after them. Sure, there's a feeling of satisfaction in purchasing a new coin to add to your collection (particularly in the case of looking for it for a long period of time). But, it doesn't necessarily mean that once you have purchased that a coin will keep its worth (or even appreciate).

Conserving and protecting collections is an vital step in the process. Without it, you're just throwing money away in the form of buying goods that aren't long-term investments or long-term pleasures.

In this section we will discuss the best ways to ensure your coins remain in mint condition for years, or even decades following their purchase. As many of these suggestions you adhere to the greater chance you'll be able to keep and increase worth of your collection.

The Toolkit You Will Need

To ensure that your collection is in tip-top condition (as as to be sure that you're making the correct purchases and, naturally) it is necessary to have the minimum toolkit you can keep on hand:

An magnifying glasses (ideally you should choose a magnifying glass that can offer 7x magnification but not over 8x). This will enable you to examine the specifics of your coins in detail.

* A notebook, a few index cards or some kind of software or application to assist you in keeping an eye on your belongings.

* A storage container that allows you to keep your belongings dry and safe.

* Cotton gloves for use for handling your money.

A reference guidebook that you can use to have a quick look at information related to coin collecting. It is also possible to utilize one of the applications we've described in the previous chapters, if it works better for your needs.

Rememberthat diligence, patience and a thirst for information are three other things you must include in the "toolkit." If you don't have those, the rest could be a failure!

How to handle Coins

A lot of new collectors aren't completely aware of this problem however, knowing how to handle coins is of utmost importance. In fact, it's crucial that it should not just be a choice, it should become instead a necessity.

The wrong handling of coins can drastically alter their value and, consequently their value. You may think it's not important to play with the coin using your fingers but your fingers may end up damaging it, especially when you do it multiple times.

What should you do with the coins you have in your collection? Here are some suggestions:

Don't touch them with your naked hands. That's what the cotton gloves are intended for.

• If the coins are stored in a holder that is specifically designed for them put them inside the holder, and don't attempt to take them out.

Be sure to grab your coins from the edges with your thumb and forefinger. Don't hold your coins by touching the surface of the front (obverse) or the back (reverse) surface because it could affect the design and quality of the quality of the.

* If you're worried that you may lose your coin while you're handling it, put it on an extremely soft and thick towel.

Be sure to not talk while you're handling your coins. These tiny drops of saliva can cause spots that are difficult to eliminate, as ridiculous as it may sound.

The coins you have aren't only "money," they are precious artifacts from the past (and the present). They are a reminder of important moments that have occurred in the past days of the past, and more then that they bring with them stories that will never be repeated. From the child who purchased an ice cream using his old coin to the grandma who given it to him collections coins are a source of excitement, joy and sorrows simultaneously.

Treat them like art. Treat them like the masterpieces of art that they are, with care, dedication and care!

How do you clean Coins

Contrary to what many believe that cleaning your coins is an essential and normal part of maintaining your collection of coins. The only reason to clean your coins is if you add circulated coins in your collections (and especially if you intend for to make this an activity that you can share with your children).

In all other situations in any other circumstance, be careful not to clean coins in any way that you can. Older coins or coins that you have inherited are often damaged through cleaning. Even if the issue is not major cleaning them could make them look old and reveal tiny scratches and cracks within the metal.

If. However, you are in the initial situation and want to get rid of circulated coins, you may clean them by following these guidelines:

*Make sure you've got all the tools in your kit including two plastic bins, one clean, soft towel as well as running tap water ruby alcohol (if you wish to) as well as some mild dishwashing detergent.

Begin by washing your hands thoroughly with soap to wash the fine grit and oils from your hands.

You can take the towel, lay it out in a folded manner several times. Make sure that it's near the containers.

*Make a bath with soap inside one of these containers making use of mild dish soap as well as the warm water from your tap. The reason to use the plastic container is because glass or metal could damage your precious coins. Be sure not to overdo it with the dish soap. You do not want to bathe your coins a complete bubble bath. You just need to ensure that you take any potential bacteria and viruses off of them.

Choose the coin that you would like to wash carefully, and then immerse it in soapy water. Carefully rub the coins' sizes between your hands with a motion which goes from the edges of the coin all the way to the middle.

*Start each one at a time. Don't include all the coins you'd like to wash into the container, since they may cause damage to one another.

*Run the coin that has been washed under warm, running tap water until soap residue has gone. Be aware that you must try to use the least amount of force is possible!

Fill the other container with distilled water , then swirl the coin around in it. This can help remove any chlorine residue or other contaminants that could cause damage to the appearance to the coins.

*Put the towel away to dry off onto the cloth. Before you store it within your collections, be sure that the coin has completely dried. In addition, as with all coins be sure to take it in your hands by the edges.

How to store Coins

Storing your coins is also important to taking care of them as it helps keep them safe from a range of elements that could harm the coins (believe you me, tiny specks of dust could be damaging over time).

To understand the reasons why it is crucial to properly store your coins You should take into consideration the following causes of damaged coins (all of that are more well-known than you think):

*Humidity. The primary source of damages to coins that are collectible. Both copper and silver cause chemical reactions in the presence of moisture, and it is true that moisture is all over. Therefore, it's extremely difficult to limit the chance of a hazard (there are methods to achieve this, but it's not certain therefore, the more careful you are the safer you'll be).

*Extreme temperatures. Insuring your coins are kept in places that are too hot can result in an increase in humidity, acidity, and air pollution (all of which can harm the coin more quickly than typical). Additionally keeping your collection in extremely low temperatures could cause condensing on the surfaces of your coins.

* Acids. It is not necessary to apply actual acids on your coins to harm them. There

are instances when storage containers and coin holders are made of cardboard or paper, and the acids that are typically used in these products can cause discoloration and toning of coins. Therefore, it is essential to stay clear of any type of storage for coins which contain acids.

* Chlorine. This harsh chemical is known to corrode coins, and can cause them to tone. Also, you don't need to dip your coins in chlorine in order to experience the effects. The majority of plastic coin holders have PVC which in reality contains chlorine in its makeup. This is why it's essential to use only coin holders that are free of PVC.

* Air pollution. The air we breathe is extremely harmful to us human beings and our environment, but it also can harm coins when it happens. Make sure to keep them from exposure to the air for as long possible (and particularly if you reside within or near a metropolitan region).

* Improper handling. As we've mentioned it is imperative to be cautious when

handling your coins as this as well can cause a lot of harm to them.

Okay, after taking all of these pieces of information into consideration, where can you put your coins?

A few options are:

*Acid-free sleeves for paper or envelopes tubes, folders album, coins or flips

*Small plastic bags made of PVC (also known as "slabs" (sealed with hard plastic) You may prefer these for most precious coins.

* To prevent tripping over your collection of coins, make sure to keep a list of every coin you own. This will allow you to ensure that you are aware of the coins you own and which coins are needed to complete a collection within your collection. Keep your list in a classic notebook or use software or an app.

Let's say that you've already chosen your storage type. Where will you place your envelopes, sleeves or slabs to ensure you shield your precious coins from potential dangers?

Be aware of these guidelines:

* Avoid high temperatures, low heats acid, salt chlorine, air pollution (as as per the suggestions we've already elaborated on earlier)

*Make sure your storage place is dark, dry, and temperature-controlled

Beware of the basement because it is extremely humid and cold.

Also, stay clear of the attic because it is often too hot and rough

Bedrooms or living room will probably be a good fit for all of the above because you're comfortable there (and because of that it is highly likely that your money can be "comfortable" too.)

Most importantly, you should make use of metal cabinets instead of wooden ones as they will be more resistant to moisture. Be sure to be aware of where you place the cabinet, too, since it may still attract moisture if, for instance the cabinet is placed near a humid wall.

There is also the option to purchase special coin cabinets. The addition of silica gel envelopes in the cabinets will allow you to keep your moisture at the optimal amounts for coins.

Also, you can keep your money in a safe deposit box, or even in an office or home safe, as these options are likely to satisfy all the requirements.

If you believe that the collection will be scrutinized frequently, make sure you select a method of storage that lets you quickly do this without taking the coins from the sleeves.

The more you do with your coins, the higher the likelihood that they'll survive the elements of time in pristine condition. Therefore, your investment will hold greater value in the years to come when (or when) it is decided to dispose of your collections.

Purchase Insurance for Your Collection

In the book, purchasing insurance for your collection of coins is the most secure, sensible and smartest plan you could come up with. What is the reason?

Insurance can protect your collection from theft or loss. If you are protected, you might be able to get back the initial investment.

Many people have their coin collections that are covered by their home insurance policy, however remember that you must double-check the policy you have in place regarding this. As an example, your collection may only be covered to $200.

If you've already started collecting costly coins, insurance is more than an "must" rather than it is a "maybe". In general, insurance firms will charge a yearly cost of 1% of the total worth of the collection. Based on the value of it is this could be a bit expensive, but the cost is well enough to be worth it.

Seven Mistakes to Avoid When preserving Your Coin Collection

To conclude this chapter, we will discuss the most popular ways that people ruin collections (some of which are very complex and expensive,). As you'll realize, many of them have been discussed within the text, however it's more than worthwhile to revisit them to show how important it is to stay clear of them.

Below are seven mistakes to avoid if you're a collector of coins:

Doing the Touch

The touch of your coins could cause tiny scratches and stains on them. This could, in turn decrease their value over time.

Cleaning them

As we have discussed previously the process of cleaning coins that you must be avoiding at all times due to the chlorine, detergent, or even the gentle rubbing could cause damage to the coins.

They are slapping them with their hands

It's true that you may not be consciously spitting onto your coin, however engaging in conversation with them could release tiny drops of saliva that could harm the coins.

Breaking their Holders

Don't do it. It won't be a good idea, but it will make them more vulnerable to become "attacked" through a myriad of dangerous elements however, you could damage the coins too (e.g. you could scratch them accidentally).

Exposing them to Acid

As I mentioned earlier there is no need to drop acid on your coins. There are times when even things that you keep your coins in might contain acids that can harm them irreparably.

Exposing them to PVC

One of the primary methods to determine the condition of a coin stored in a PVC sleeves is by the green slime that is on the top. It is not a good idea to have to see that on your coins, so stay clear of PVC as often as you can!

Exposing them to harmful elements

The weather, rain, snow and cold, anything that can be harmful to your health or discomforting could likely impact your coins too. Be sure to keep them as safe and sealed as you can!

These things may seem simple but the truth is that they're absolutely the most prevalent and frequent issues in the field of damage to coins. If you take every precaution to avoid these issues, you'll be able to reduce the possibility that something negative occurs to your valuable collection.

There is no way to completely ensure your coins are safe from damage of any kind however you can make a difference to avoid the most common catastrophes. The way I've described it previously: treat your coins as something you truly love and cherish, not only an "business occasion" which will allow you to earn more money. Once you begin to shift your mental outlook to this kind of attitude, you'll naturally be more aware of your collection from different viewpoints.

It is crucial to recognize that you can't be in control of all things. It is impossible to be in control of the way your money is treated over the course of two, three or even four decades, since many factors could cause damage in on a different way.

What you are able to manage However, it is worthwhile to invest in as it can significantly reduce the risk and boost worth of the collection.

Chapter 7: Making Money

Like I said in the previous chapters, coin collecting could be a profitable business. Many people view their collection of coins as more than just a hobby, and use them as investment opportunities to the future.

The ability to earn money from coins is not an investment that you can be expecting instant ROI. There is a time frame for coins to increase in value. It is also a level of expertise to determine which coins to buy and when to sell them, and the best way to dispose of them in order to make the highest profits.

Don't fret, however. It's an issue that of perseverance (which I have been encouraging throughout the entire book). For skill, it is exactly what we've been discussing throughout the book. Yes, it takes some time to understand the fundamentals of collecting coins (and selling) however it is able to be accomplished, without doubt.

In this section, we'll explore the idea of earning profits from your collection of coins. We will cover starting with A-Z, the important things you need to consider when trying selling your collections to make profits such as price guides as well as money-making strategies that collectors employ and how to comprehend the market for coins and more.

Let's roll!

How to determine the value of the Coin

Understanding how to price your coins is not only from the standpoint of profit but also from the viewpoint of how buyers think about your company. In the case of pricing a coin too low could raise suspicions, and make buyers believe you're trying to scam them. In the same way, overpricing a currency could either turn them off (because it's outside the budget) or cause them to believe that you are trying to steal their money.

To figure out the value of an item, you must first be reminded of the features that make it valuable: rarity material demand, and all that we have previously mentioned in the earlier chapters.

Furthermore it is highly suggested that you consult the price Guide to get an overall understanding of current prices and values. Potential buyers can get an understanding of the market, which will to ensure that you're on the same level.

A couple of Price Guides you may want to look over include:

* PCGS Price Guide

* NGC Coin Price Guide

* NGC World Gold Coin Price Guide Coinflation (which provides the melt values of coins)

* Coin Dealer Newsletter

* Heritage Price Guide for Beginners

* Heritage Price Guide for Numismatists

* Coin Archives

*The Red Book Online

* British Coin Price Guide

* U.S. Currency Price Guide

* Prices for Econols

There are numerous other sources similar to this however, whichever one you pick, you must make sure that it is checked in the eyes of the general public, and it is a reliable sources of info.

Be aware that the prices of coins are not simply "invented". As with most markets around the world, they're dependent on the dynamic between demand and supply. If there's only a few unique coins that are of the same sort that are available on the market it is likely that they will cost more. If there are a lot of coins, price will decrease.

Being able to read the market and be able to make informed guesses about the future is vital if you are looking to earn a money. This is the same for the majority of types of investments in actual. For instance, if you decide to invest in stocks, you'll be required to learn about the fluctuations of the market in order to determine the best time to purchase as well as the best time to sell.

We'll discuss further the changing trends of the cryptocurrency market and the best way to understand it in the next section of this chapter. For now, let's take a look at a very important issue...

Strategies for Money Making Employed by Coin Collectors

Alongside knowing how to value your coins (and finding the best time to sell) You should also be aware of the different strategies used by collectors in the marketplace.

While there are a myriad of strategies, these five are the most common (and generally effective):

Buy and hold

This is among the most well-known methods for earning money from your collection of coins. Similar to the example of stock shown earlier the strategy involves purchasing coins, storing until they appreciate in value and later selling the coins. The majority times this method is appropriate for those who plan to stay in the game for a long time (such as those who consider investing in coins as part of their retirement portfolio, as an instance).

Buy Blue Chips

Blue Chips are the kind of coins that attract a huge appeal to a wide audience and are constantly increasing in value. They are generally very sought-after among collectors of coins that vary from beginners to expert. They are comparatively scarce but they continue growing in value each year.

Blue chips are a excellent long-term option for those who don't want to reap profits in a hurry. It is possible to make a profit within the next two or three years however, in these scenarios the longer you sit longer, the better profits you could earn.

Be aware of the Inflection Points

This is a similar strategy to investing in momentum stocks and is generally advised for investors and collectors with a little knowledge in the field.

The strategy is (very) short the short term, this strategy involves purchasing at the lower end from rising points of inflection. These are the points (or grades) where the demand is high and this pushes up retail cost (sometimes even double the price). If you can anticipate when this will happen and you are able to wait for the right time to sell your coins at an extremely high yield.

Remember that this may not be the case for very high-grade coins (such as those that are not circulated). This is that the market thinks that these coins are fair valued.

Make use of a large collector base

This approach involves searching for, purchasing, and selling coins that are priced at a reasonable price for the typical collector. Because this broadens your market and increase the chance that you'll be capable of selling your coins quicker and earn profit. The amount you earn for every coin you sell may not be huge however, if you apply the sale to several coins, you could get a fairly decent amount of cash from it.

Cherry Pick

This is the exact opposite of the previous one. Simply, cherry-picking coins involves choosing a small target market and attempting to get the most of the movement of the coin (which we'll discuss in the following part of the chapter). By purchasing when prices are the lowest and then identifying your market at exactly the time when prices hit their peak, you can quickly make a substantial profit from your coin-selling activities.

If you are a novice it is possible to begin with an extensive collection base, and later "upgrade" to more advanced methods. All of them can bring returns, but keep in mind that there's never 100% certain for any investment (stocks or entrepreneurs, coins the list is endless). Plan for the best and being prepared for the worst is therefore, the most effective method to follow no matter the kind of investments you may be thinking about.

Knowing the Coin Market

Understanding your costs and strategy is just one aspect, but you're doing this "game" entirely on your on your own. In reality the performance of your investment will be determined in part by the movements in the marketplace.

Therefore, being at the very least familiar with the way that markets move will help you make better choices both in regards to purchasing as well as when it comes to trading your currency.

These are the cycles of the Coin Market

The market for coin is fairly simple to grasp because it is largely dependent on demand and supply. The supply is restricted and is determined by the government issuing the coins, and the demand fluctuates and can be affected by various aspects.

Let's suppose there are 50 pieces of a particular coin. When there's 100 people who want to buy it for it, the price will rise. If there are only 40 buyers, it will drop. If somebody (an organization, for instance) decides to market the coin and exaggerate its value, the it is likely that the amount of buyers will increase multiple times (depending on how effective the marketing campaign was). If this happens it is a sign that the market is not balanced and the value of the coin could rise dramatically.

What's even more fascinating is that, if the price of a coin is premium price, other coins that are adjacent to it will likely to adjust to the market.

Let's look at a specific instance. Silver Dollar from 1974. Silver Dollar sold for no less than $10 million, the sort of amount that was big enough (and likely shocking enough) to break out of the circle of collectors and into the mainstream media (Reaney 2013).

In the end, the interest rate for the entire Mint State Bank Dollars soared in a matter of hours and they became useful (even even if they were less graded). An experienced investor will know however that this is an interim state, so they'd either seize the opportunity and purchase prior to the interest wave increases or overlook the chance and search for a coin which follows the same pattern.

It's a lot as gambling but the reality is that the market for coins is much more reliable than Russian Roulette or a game of Poker. It's not always easy to "smell" the perfect possibility however when you can, it will surely bring you back.

How to Handle It

Three main elements that influence the demand for a coin that can affect the demand for a coin: the price of silver and gold as well as speculation and the trends (we have already talked about several of these at the start of this book).

If you're looking to play the safest game it is best to always look into opportunities that are long-term. They may not bring the kinds of huge returns you see on television however, they are an investment that is safe and can allow you to retire knowing that your investments are safe. The same principle applies to all of the investments in the portfolio of yours, way, not just to coins.

Naturally, there are times when you may consider tapping into opportunities in the short term however, as a standard of practice it is not recommended to depend too heavily on them. Think like a collector instead of those who want to earn cash quickly. Consider buying like an investor But try to consider the long-term impact of the investments you make in.

Selling Your Coins

Selling your coins must be handled with care. By following the guidelines mentioned earlier in this chapter, and your experience with the currency that you are selling, try to ensure that the transaction is beneficial to you.

It is therefore crucial to not be pressured to sell-not because you're facing financial difficulties, but because your market is looking dim. The right timing to sell is essential. For instance some experts advise selling during the months of January, July or even August (which coincides with when largest coin shows are held).

If you decide to market them the coins, you can boost the value of your coins when you make them appear attractive. That doesn't mean you need to scrub or treat them! But cleaning them can aid.

Additionally is that you must also get your coins verified through CAC (the Certified Acceptance Corporation). This will increase your credibility with the buyer , and also assist you in avoiding the risk of undergrading (which is a technique used whereby unethical sellers as well as experts in grading deliberately reduce the value of a coin sold by a seller in order to purchase it for lower prices).

Furthermore it would be fantastic to have your coins attributed. This can be done quickly if you utilize the attribution service offered by NGC.

If you're going to an event, ensure that you display your coins in a positive light and present your booth in a way that is appealing to all. In addition, it is recommended to have at least three bids from dealers because this can help you to fight offers that are too expensive.

They are, naturally some general guidelines. Keep in mind that trustworthiness, professionalism and grade, as well as accreditation, all can help make your offer more convincing to prospective buyers.

Imagine yourself as someone looking for coins, and not selling something: what could bring you to purchase your product? Rereading the chapter 3 of this text may aid you a bit by helping you refresh the most important factors to be considered when purchasing coin (which also are requirements that you need to meet as an entrepreneur, too).

Where can You sell your Coins?

There are many options for you to market your coin. In essence, there's any "right" nor "wrong" option to sell your coins. The goal is to allow you to target your customers, so you're likely to be looking for places that have a more niche appeal.

For example, selling your coins in a flea market could not yield a profit because the people who attend aren't necessarily in search of coins (and therefore, they might not understand the value of the coin that you are putting up to sell).

What are the best places to sell them what do you do?

Here are a few options to consider:

* To a dealer. Most often, you'll receive a lower cost from a dealer since they want to take the coin in the future (and make

money from the process, too). However selling the coin to a dealer is the most secure and fastest method to go about it. Additionally, if your dealer has offered you an assurance to buy back that is still in effect, you may be able to get the market value of the coin.

* To a coin shop. Like in the case of dealers the coin shop can be a disadvantage since you will most likely not get the best value for your coins in this location.

* to a pawnshop. Based on the value of the coin and its rarity the pawn shop may be willing to purchase the item from you. Of course, the cost may be much lower than the price of the market due to the fact that the pawnshop might be required to pay for appraisals and also be able to profit from the whole deal.

* To a coin show. Contrary to the three previous scenarios, a coin show is likely to offer you more control over the cost. Naturally, you should not over- or under-

value your coins. However, an organized show can allow you to show your merchandise to people who are interested in collecting coins.

* Online. There are numerous options for you to market your coin on the internet. Generalist websites such as eBay or Amazon permit you to sell your coins (either through auctions or directly selling). Additionally, there are special online auction or commerce websites that sell coins and other collectibles. It's probably best to consider selling your coins through these websites (for this reason, too)., you should never sell items at an auction or flea marketplace and not at a professional show like a coin show, for instance.).

• On forum and other social media. It is true that the Internet is a huge area, which means you can discover forums and groups with a focus on collecting coins. Make sure you're prepared to provide anyone who might be interested with all the information about your coins, to ensure you can attest to its authenticity!

* Refineries and smelters. If you are looking to melt your coins for valuable metal head to a refinery or smelter. This is usually only recommended in cases where the coins themselves do not offer any significant worth (e.g. it's of a low quality) however, you need to recoup your investment (and earn a profits) through melting its precious metal.

The idea of meeting with collectors from your peer group and offering their coins is an feasible option. But, ensure that you set sensible boundaries, especially in the case of being close to them (otherwise you may find yourself selling the coin at a lesser price simply because you don't feel comfortable giving a friend a discount).

Sorts of Coins Selling to be aware of

If you go through the above list you'll be able to draw the following conclusion in a clear manner that there are three primary kinds of locations that you can purchase coins.

* Private sales that are direct and private (such such as selling at a coin fair or on Amazon or a specific website). The main benefit of this kind selling is the fact that you receive immediate payment (which could be something worth thinking about particularly if your research suggests that the value of your coins will decrease within a shorter time).

* Consignment (which means that you'll leave your currency at your dealer's location and ask the dealer to sell it under the name of your company). In exchange for the service, the dealer will earn the commission. In the end you must be aware that consignment sales probably take a long time to pay you the cash. Additionally, it is very important to locate an individual you can count on with your money and believe that they will give you a fair price.

Auctions, which may be classified as private or public. The auctions that are public are, as their name implies accessible to all. Contrarily, private auctions are restricted to a limited number of. You can select a specialist auction house, or you can auction with your dealer or you can sell your coins through auction sites on the internet (such like eBay for instance).

Chapter 8: How to Purchase Coins

If you're a new coin collector seeking out older coins, the number of options is overwhelming. eBay and online coin dealers and brick-and-mortar shops for coins are just a few examples of the most sought-after collectible coin stores available.

How do you determine where to look for old coins? In this article, I'll discuss both the benefits and drawbacks of searching for coins from each source.

eBay

eBay is the most popular marketplace for collecting coins. On eBay there is a wide selection of items from vintage U.S. coins to world coins, including silver and gold bullion.

What is it that makes eBay ideal for coin buyers is the fact the fact that prices are usually lower than retail--i.e. less than you'd expect to pay if purchased a coin from a dealer. This means that lots of bargains are available.

One of the advantages of eBay is its huge variety. If you're not interested in the most specific and narrow segment, chances are you'll be able to locate what you're seeking on eBay.

The biggest drawback to eBay can be the clear drawback of purchasing a coin isn't visible in person. It's difficult to judge the authenticity (and maybe even authenticity) that a particular coin is simply looking at a photograph of it. This issue is exacerbated by poor quality photos and shady sellers.

If you're a novice collector only beginning to explore collecting I don't suggest jumping into the depths of eBay at first. Begin by buying smaller amounts of coins from sellers that have excellent ratings on feedback (i.e. 99.9 to 100 percent) and many transactions.

Once you've gained a greater understanding of the types of sellers that are trustworthyand which the image relates to a coin that is in hand and you are ready exploring the more costly and scarce collector's coins.

Coin Shops

Do you feel uncomfortable purchasing online? Another good place to purchase old coins is at your nearby coinshop. Every decent-sized city is likely to be home to one of them shops, although it's possible that they could be more of an amalgamation of a coin shop and jewelry.

I recommend that you take one look at Yelp reviews before visiting the latest coin shop. Do not let a couple of negative reviews deter you from making the trip to the store, but do keep any negative customer reviews at the forefront of your head while you look over the selection of items available.

It isn't realistic to expect prices that are comparable to those on eBay in an ordinary shop selling coins, because the costs associated with running a brick-and-mortar retail store must be factored into the coins price. But , you are likely to locate the majority of U.S. coins, and likely some world coins that are cheap also.

Be aware that counterfeit coins could be a concern in stores that are involved in dealing with a large amount of inventory, which means they might not have the enough time to authenticate every coin prior to putting it up to be sold.

"Caveat empty of guilt" is the rule here. Coin shops rarely label coins that have been damaged or cleaned. Examine any coin prior to buying it at least with some form of magnifying. In the next section of this book I will go over the indicators that you should look for in order to tell whether a coin has been cleaned.

Online Coin Dealers

Due to the popularity of the internet and eCommerce increasingly, dealers are selling their coins online. National dealers such as APMEX and Littleton provide a variety of options but not with prices as affordable as eBay.

Coin dealers who are independent like me specialize in particular areas, and often have greater catalogs for these areas than can be available on eBay.

Do you know a seller whom you love on eBay? Try one quick Google search for the seller's name to determine whether they have their own website. A lot of the bigger sellers do. You'll see the same items they sell on eBay with lower prices on their site due to the absence of selling costs.

Coin Auction Houses

As you advance in the hobby, you could be drawn towards more valuable coins. Auction houses such as Heritage Auctions, GreatCollections, and Stack's Bowers offer rarer and more valuable coins than the ones you can discover on eBay. Be aware that bidding is typically fierce, and the coins are sold at expensive prices. Another thing to note is that a lot of auction house (unlike eBay) have a "buyer's premium" charge of 15% on top of the amount of money that is paid out at auction.

Coin Roll Hunting

Are you on a tight budget? Have no fear! All you need to do is visit the bank in your area and swap your cash to a couple of coins. When you come across something that is valuable you can replace it with the normal coin and then return your money to your bank. The total cost is very low but the thrill of the hunt is an enjoyable experience.

Some valuable coins to search for are quarters, silver dimes and half dollars prior to 1964 (these coins were made with 90 percent silver alloy instead of copper nickel); Lincoln Wheat cents prior to 1958 as well as Kennedy quarter dollars dating from 1965 to 1970 (produced in 40 percent sterling alloy).

The majority of coin roll enthusiasts believe that quarter rolls are being sorted out pretty well by now which is why you should limit yourself to dime and half dollar coins for silver as well as penny rolls to collect Wheat cents. It is recommended to make friends with your local bank cashier or teller is suggested as they might be able to identify and put aside some intriguing coin rolls for you. Another suggestion is to check the reject slot on Coinstar machines, since silver coins may be turned away by machines because of their weight, and often left in there.

Best practices for buying Coins

Learn what you can from the people you know.

Many new collectors are attracted by an "great bargain" on coins they have nothing about. Unfortunately, good deals in the world of coin collecting are rare and hard to come by The majority of sellers are aware of what they own and will price it accordingly.

This is in line with the number 1 of our five Principles of Coin Collecting, "Buy the book prior to you purchase an item." The power of knowledge is and it is beneficial greatly to have at the very least an understanding of the market price as well as rarity and methods of grading before buying the coin.

I realize that this could sometimes be a challenge to make a commitment to, and I'm not ashamed to admit that I do not always adhere to what I say. Sometimes I'll come to a nice-looking coin I simply must own and I'm sure that I know little about it.

If that occurs, I'll quickly search eBay to find out what similar coins are worth, or have sold for previously. Also, I'll limit myself to coins that are less expensive as I'm not willing spend $500 on a coin that I don't know anything about. It could be worth it to solicit the seller to hold the coin for you Many will do this and provide you with a few extra days to investigation.

Take the time to study the coin

It may seem like normal sense, but be sure to examine the coin on both sides.

If you purchase online, this involves looking at all of the images and inspecting the surface. If the images are blurry or cropped, you can contact the seller to request better photos. Be aware that the seller could attempt to hide some information by using poor photos.

If you are viewing photos online make sure you zoom in as far as possible to see whether the seller has altered the photos . The most common techniques for editing photos include:

Editing out a scratch or mark by copying another area on the surface of the coin before placing it over the scratch.

The increase in the saturation of the color can increase the color of the coin to make it appear more vibrant - this is a major issue for coins with tone. It's usually discovered through looking into the colors of other areas in the image like the background, and determining if they appear normal or bright.

The camera is not properly white balanced. camera prior to taking a picture (usually not intentional) which causes the color of the coin appear to be out of. Like with saturation, you should look at other areas of the image to find out if the color is natural. Silver coins are generally like silver or grey and gold coins should appear yellow/orange or gold.

Zooming out or taking an cropped photo makes the actual coin extremely small and difficult to spot.

If you spot one of these consider whether you actually are interested in buying the coin . The seller could be hiding some kind of information or trying create the appear more attractive than it really is.

If purchasing in person, take the coin or holder to the edge (see for more information in the next chapter about what to do with coins) and turn it around to be able to catch light. This will identify any minor scratch marks or scratches that would otherwise be missed as well as expose any mint luster that remains in the coins.

Make use of a jeweler's loupe, or a small magnifying glasses to get an in-depth view of the surface. I usually recommend five or 10x magnifying loupe for jewelers and it will cost approximately $11 for it on Amazon or at the nearest coin shop. The use of a loupe is a permissible in the coin shop or at a coin exhibition, and any dealer who refuses to look at that exact glance could be trying to hide something.

Chapter 9: Grading Services

There are many grading companies accessible today which provide a wide range of services. These include experts in the field taking a look at your coins to determine the Mint State (MS) or to authenticate and assess your collection of collectibles. The range of services includes old currency, Baseball cards, comics, and coins. If it's an item of interest, there is an evaluation service for it.

Grading is a crucial service If an item is not graded, it will be unsuitable for auction or sale won't fetch the price when it's sold. If, however , you decide to spend the time and some cash to get the item graded, then the item can be sold at a higher price in the future. Grading services allow buyers and collectors to feel confident and be certain they are buying genuine and not a fake. There are numerous counterfeit items in circulation and it's difficult to determine if an item is authentic or not.

There are many grading companies and secondary grading companies that will eliminate all the guesswork out of proving the authenticity of the object you'd like to acquire to add to your collection or sell to a third party. The services I have listed are considered to be the top available the moment and can fetch higher prices after a coin has been graded by these sources. The top two grading organizations on the market today comprise Numismatic Guarantee Corporation, also known as NGC as well as Profession Coin Grading Service or PCGS. These two services typically offer better prices since they've become the most popular and reliable businesses for grading.

There are many others which offer excellent graders, but they do not offer the most competitive prices when they grade by these firms. These are companies worth a look and you might be pleasantly surprised to discover that working with them could be more advantageous to your pocketbook or even more than you would like. These grading services include, but aren't restricted to: Independent Coin Graders (IGC), The American Numismatic Association Certification Service (ANACS, according to their website, is the oldest grader in America), Star Grading Service (SEGS) and other services. I'll include websites for these services to allow you to conduct your own research before choosing which grading service is the best fit for your needs.

There are other secondary grading services available. What these secondary grading companies do is to check the item again to confirm that the product is authentic and provides a further level of protection to all buyers as well as collectors and sellers alike. The one you'll notice the most is represented with a green oval, or CAC bean, as collectors have been known to call it the Certified Acceptance Corporation (CAC). A grading service that is top-quality and the CAC stickers in the shape of a green means that the coin went through multiple layers of interspersed grading. You can purchase it with confidence knowing that the coin is of the grade it is and has been checked multiple times. CAC is by far the sole secondary grader I've come across however I believe that more secondary grading services could be in the pipeline or may be coming soon.

If you own a coin that you'd like be graded, visit the sites that are listed under the section on notes in the end in the volume. Each company are going to have different submission requirements and guidelines. The majority of these companies require you sign up , and move on to the next one. Pricing and other details can be found on their own websites. It is also possible to attend an exhibition of coins. Most of the top grading companies were discovered when I went to the bigger coin shows. I joined for a year with NGC for approximately $200. Part of the cost was used to pay for grading services and grading services. Grading cost about $30 per coin. But, prices fluctuate constantly and you can also avoid the whole process altogether by contacting an individual dealer in your area as well as paying them for the privilege to submit the coin for you. It is also possible to purchase pre-graded coins.

Chapter 10: Gold Coin Collecting

The art of collecting coins began in the early days when coins were initially issued to facilitate trade. It was only during the Middle Ages that people turned this into a pastime because of the artwork and historical significance.

The art of collecting coins is an activity that many people enjoy. Some of the most valuable and costly collections can be owned by anyone is the gold coins. Gold's most valuable coin that anyone has ever purchased was valued at around $8 million. It coin was known as known as the American 1933 Gold Eagle. This is why the collection of gold coins should be called the pastime of kings.

Gold coins were among the earliest forms of money. Later, they were then followed by the silver coin. Gold coins were available throughout the Us between 1838 and 1933. They were stocked with that of the Liberty Head bust but this was only introduced in 1907. The design was later altered to incorporate it's Indian Head and Saint Gaudens designs and continued to be in use until 1933 in the year that it was the time that Fantastic Depression began. This led to the recall of gold coins , which make them difficult to locate today.

Since they are not in use anymore and are no longer in circulation, the cost of these rare commodities is very expensive. Gold is used to make different things like jewelry or bars that are kept for investment purposes.

South Africa minted its first gold Krugerrand coin in the year 1967. The coin is not a face value and is only used as an emblem. It is composed of one an ounce of gold. It could be purchased to invest in.

Since then, several countries have produced bullion-based coins. Canada created their Gold Maple Leaf in 1979 and Australia created its Nugget on the 1st of January, 1981. Both are significantly more popular over that of South African coin since of its purity of 24 carats.

A lot of people hold gold as a form of investment as they think that the increased demand for gold will cause its value to grow. Some view it as insurance in case the financial conditions get more dire. There was a the past where the more paper currency produced more expensive the cost of gold, which kept cash and gold at the same worth. After the standard came to an end in 1971, it was possible for the government to create more paper currency, without increasing the cost of gold.

Since gold coins cannot be used to purchase merchandise, the majority of coin collectors keep them in their collections to remind themselves of how they were once utilized by people.

Chapter 11: The Way To collect Coins Like a Pro

Being a professional coin collector requires you to think about various things differently. One of the first things an experienced coin collector needs to learn is to determine the worth of a coin.

Let's take a look at how to tell if this coin is worthy of the space in your wallet or not.

Evaluation of the Value of a Coin

Now, your suspicion is that you've got all the tools listed already in place. However, regardless of how skilled your eyes are they are unable to determine the worth of a coin without assistance.

The process of evaluating the value of a piece of coin is dependent on the grading of coins that we discussed in greater detail in our book. You can use that system as a beginner-friendly-getting-started-point,
but there are others ways to check the coin's value once you collect it.

Below are the numismatists' components they employ to assess the value of a coin:

Luster: Luster coins is typically how well the coin can reflect light falling on its surface. The sharper the reflection of light is, the more attractive the coin's shines. Coins that have a good luster usually have higher worth. That's why the one classified 70 in the Sheldon Scale has perfect luster.

Color: This could result in the form of coloration from the material used to make the coin as well as the intensity of any other colorization included in the design. When you are evaluating coins for value, make sure to examine the color of the metal (golden or silver colored coins typically sell for more) and any additional color that is that is added by design.

Contact Marks: as we've seen the coins that were circulated will usually have many contact marks, which are also known as detracting marks. The marks are usually caused by inadequate handling, and fingerprints being referred to as detracting marks. Coins that have more marks can fetch lower prices however, this could depend on other aspects for instance, the metal's value.

Eye Appeal: Although this may sound like something that is personal to you However, there are ways to determine if that a coin has great eye appeal. It is the absence of major defects, vinyl damageor the absence of carbon streaks as well as other indicators.

Rare coins always fetch more. That's why commemorative coins and coins like U.S. Gold Coin are highly sought-after objects. Rareness increases the value of a coin and popularity. It could be valid even if the coin has obvious marks. However, the worth of a rare coin may decline if it is not properly stored and stored so that it is not rated highly according to the Sheldon Scale. This isn't the case, because rare coins rarely circulate at all, meaning that they're almost always perfect.

Bullion: Since bullion is a way of looking at intrinsic worth of coins, rather than their face value, it's an effective method of determining the worth of a coin. Bullion coins facilitate the easier and more efficient sales of precious metals like silver and gold. For instance the present value for 1 oz of American Eagle (with about 31.104 grams of pure gold) is $1800 and $2100. While the price for pure gold is $1960. Bullions are also secure and reliable storage.

mint marks: as we observed in the "S mint mark" coins when a mint is out of production or ceases producing coins, coins with the mint mark are assumed to have an increased value. Also, similar to coins with no mint mark No Mint mark coins, an error could also cause a coin to have no mint mark is worth more.

Market Psychology Market psychology is a term used by the financial market to the emotional state of participants. It is the general feeling that people who are part of the market to purchase or sell their shares because they feel certain.

When it comes to coin collection This would mean that collectors of coins would seek out coins on the basis of conviction that they possess an intrinsic worth. This is dependent on knowing the history of the coin and its appearance and other aspects.

Now that you are aware of the crucial metrics you need to concentrate on to assess the worth of a coin, what coins should you be looking for when you get to work?

The Most Popular Coins To Begin With

The below coins are well-known and are still highly valuable because of their past or their metal or both.

#: Peace Dollar

The silver coin was created by Anthony Defrancisci and produced in 1921. It was a commemorative item designed to honor the peace that came after this Great War. It isn't rare however it is considered to be rare. As a novice you can get it for a reasonable price. The coins typically include an MS-63 collectible grade, and an MS-65 Ideal Investment grade.

#: Morgan Silver Dollar

It is the one-dollar coin that is most well-liked by collectors. This coin was issued after the passage of the Bland-Allison Act in 1878. The Act required the purchase in large quantities of silver for the production of coins.

George T Morgan designed the coin with the intent to make it half. However, they altered the design and made it an actual silver dollar in 1878.

The 1878-CC isn't scarce as Carson City in Nevada having produced two million. But it's popular, especially because it's part of the dollar coin that was the most valuable coins of its kind in U.S. history. It is possible to purchase some circulated coins at reasonable prices, however the coins that are not circulated could are more expensive.

#: Liberty Seated Dollar Coins

The dollar was first minted in 1840, and became the first coins issued in the U.S. to have patriotic themes. These coins were very popular during their day. But they were then scarce because they were created during a period when people accumulated silver to gain economic gain. The fact that silver was available in a limited quantity caused a limited manufacturing of this coin which resulted in the scarcity.

#: Saint-Gaudens Double Eagle

The coins were produced between 1907 and 1933 and have a unique story to tell. These gold coins are of the most sought-after coins that collectors can find today, and hold an important spot within the public. These coins only had a short existence due to the fact that in 1933 the US government stopped selling them due to they were deemed to be part of the Great Depression bit. In their day they were greeted with great enthusiasm by the public prior to the time that Franklin Roosevelt recalled them in 1933. This coin is worthy of having within your collections.

#: Silver and Gold Maple Leaf coins

The Canadian coins are extremely popular among Canadian Coin collectors, but they are now popular across America. United States too. With a maple leaf as well as the picture of Queen Elizabeth 2 on the reverse, this coin pays tribute to Canada's past and is sure to be a part of your collection.

#: Washington Quarter

The Washington Quarter is a 25-cent US coin that was first introduced in 1932 following designs created by John Flanagan. The coin is made of silver. Washington Quarter was minted by the Philadelphia mint. The first coins had the mint mark of 'P' on the coins. The coin is adorned with the image of the president George Washington and is another important coin to acquire.

#: Kennedy Half Dollars

The 50-cent coin first appeared in 1964 as a commemoration of the assassination the then US the president John F Kennedy, authorized within a month of Kennedy's death. The coin's production process began in January of 1964 and the remains in circulation until today.

This is certainly an item to be studied for those who are just beginning their journey.

Coins to commemorate the memory of a loved one.

As previously mentioned the term commemorative coin refers to coins designed to commemorate special occasions within the US. The range of coins that fall into this category suggests that coins are extremely valuable to many collectors of coins.

A few commemorative coins to be thinking about adding to your collection of coins include:

#: George Washington 250th Anniversary half-dollar

This coin was designed to commemorate George Washington's 250th birthday anniversary in the year of his birth. The coin was created in 1982, and is an excellent coin to have having within your collections.

#: 1983 Olympics Commemorative Silver Dollar

The coin was designed in 1984 to commemorate the Olympics which were held at Los Angeles, California. It was the first commemorative commemorative silver coin to be issued in the US since the year 1900. These coins have all three marks of the mint: P, D, and S mint marks.

1984 Olympic Silver Dollar

It was also the first coin that the US that was issued to commemorate an Olympiad held in Los Angeles. Similar to other coins, Philadelphia, Denver, and San Francisco mints all produced this coin.

The coin had an Olympic Gateway on reverse, in contrast to the discus throwing device on the coin's first one. It is now an important collectible for coin collectors.

1986 Statue of Liberty

This coin was created in honor of that of the Statue of Liberty in New York.

The reverse of the coin included on the reverse was Statue of Liberty, which was prominently displayed with the sun shining into the background. The reverse featured four figures who looked like they had recently arrived on the shores of New York, possibly immigrants. The coin is also a highly collectible item.

Error Coins That Are Worth Collecting

Error coins are popular among collectors as well. These coins are known for their mistakes on the coins, be it in the text or image on the coin or any other error that could occur.

The most well-known errors in coins include:

1971 Lincoln Cent with Double Die Obverse

"AM'" Wide 1999 reverse Lincoln Cent

No Mint Roosevelt Dime and

The 1996 Double Die Obverse Lincoln Coin.

We've examined all these except for the Lincoln Double Die of 1995 Obverse that we will take a look at below.

#: 1995 Double Die Obverse Lincoln Coin

This coin was the final of its kind following its release in the Denver as well as the Philadelphia mints adopted the single hub method. This meant they only struck only once, eliminating the risk that double-die coins carry.

The Doublestrike on this coin was clearly visible around the edges.

Wrong Planchet Mule Coins To Collect

A mule is a type of coin which is the result of two die strikes that are not intended to go together on the coin. These coins are highly sought-after and can be useful to someone who is just starting out.

We have here the 1864 2-cent piece that saw the strike place an inscription of two cents on the reverse of the coin instead of the Indian head that was supposed to be on the reverse.

Clipped planchet

A clipped planchet is a type of coin that has a small portion the edge missing because of the cracking in the planechet. These kinds of errors usually occur when the planchet went by the press for blanking. Because of inadequate feeding or speed fluctuations, some coins would be removed before the next set had completely passed. This resulted in some coins having a small portion of their metal cut off.

One example can be seen in one of these is D-Clipped Planchet Lincoln, which included a portion of the edge that was clipped to the side.

#: 1909-S VDB Lincoln Cent

The 1909 coin was designed in commemoration of the 100th anniversary of U.S. President Abraham Lincoln. Victor David Brenner, who created the coin, placed his initials, VDB, at the bottomof the coin, which distinguished himself from other coin makers who simply put initials on your last names. Only 484,000 coins were made by the San Francisco Mint.

Some of the coins were missing the VDB initials taken off, which created an instant shortage. Given that many coin collectors start their hunt for coins with Lincolns however, this is the most difficult to find. To many collectors of coins, the 1909-S VDB Lincoln Cent is considered to be the most sought-after item of coin collections, typically the last to be found for many. It has held its worth and prestige throughout the many years.

While it isn't straightforward to collect however, it's definitely an investment worthy of the time and effort.

Chapter 12: The Fundamentals of Coin Collecting

Coin collecting is believed as one of the "Hobby of the Kings." Coin collecting is distinct from hoarding money. The art of collecting coins in its current is a practice that dates through the 14th century. People across the globe collect coins. Many keep it because of their value and a lot of people just enjoy the sheer pleasure they can have by having a collection of diverse coins.

If someone is keen on making the hobby of collecting coins a passion and enjoys it, then he can achieve this. It's a pastime that does not require a particular expertise and could be performed by anyone.

There are a variety coins collectors. There are those who just enjoy it while others take it more seriously.

Informal coin collection

The majority of coin collectors, especially those who are children, begin as casual coin collectors. They are casual collectors who do not have a specific goal in the collecting of coins. They can collect coins from various nations or from different times without taking it seriously.

Coin collecting with curiosity

When the coin collector who is not a professional begins to notice the particulars that the coin has, they become an avid coin collector. A coin collector like this will not be averse to paying for coins. He simply wants to appreciate the coins. Soon, he'll start to store them in containers or albums.

Advanced coin collection

A skilled coin collector would collect coins with a specific goal in the mind. They might wish to find coins from a particular country, or even a certain period of time.

There are numerous tracks collectors of coins follow in their pastime. Here are some of the methods one can utilize when collecting coins:

Coin collection based on the nation of origin

Many coin collectors want to have a collection of coins from a certain country for a certain amount of time. This kind of collection allows the collector to travel around the world with coins. Some people may want collecting coins of the countries they have been to.

Coin collection from the past

Another method of collecting coins is to keep into consideration the the past. Coin collectors often engage in collecting coins during a specific period of history, like declarations of independence or wars.

Coins with errors

Some people like collecting coins that have errors fascinating, since these kinds of coins are very rare these days.

There are a variety of ways to accumulate coins and every one is just as entertaining as the others. It is important to experience the hobby before deciding whether to continue with it or not. The hobby of collecting coins can require specific quantities of money and the person collecting the coins must be savvy when taking part in this kind of hobby.

Purchase of Coins

There are many places where these "special coins" can be bought. These are the most basic methods and locations to acquire the coin(s) you've long dreamed of.

Go local

Coin shops are everywhere across the United States. In most cases, your neighborhood or city may have coin shops you can visit to determine whether they have any coins you'd like for your own collection. The majority of these shops are situated in larger towns or in cities. Better yet, consult the phone book of your local area and begin walking your hands through those pages determine the location of the closest cashier shop(s) is...

The shops offer coin collectors with the chance to examine and scrutinize the coins you are interested in. It is good to know that these stores are also brimming with experts and enthusiasts for coins who share your enthusiasm and are able to provide their unbiased opinions on a coin's worth or quality. They may also offer useful ideas and suggestions.

The local coin shops may have a small inventory or collection of coins and the prices they sell the coins for may be slightly higher than normal. This usually happens to collectors.

Auctions for coins

There are auctions that are specifically for coins. This is an effective, if not a great option to purchase coins. It is vital that prior to going to an auction, you understand the procedures and rules applicable.

There are many kinds of auctions, including auctions that are bidding via internet, mail and auctions that are conducted over the telephone. Be alert and watchful! It is crucial to ensure that you have fix a price for the item you plan to buy. Auctions can become very emotionally and aggressive. Make sure you are disciplined and do your best not to exceed the maximum price you've established for yourself.

Mail-ordering coins for purchase

This is a efficient and affordable method to purchase coins. Many dealers who deal via mail usually have overhead expenses that are very low, so they are able to provide identically low prices for coins that they offer.

Make sure you thoroughly review the policies of a particular dealer prior to making a return. When you receive your item, you immediately examine it for damage or authenticity. The currency you're receiving is exactly as the one you purchased and exactly as you expected.

In conclusion, purchasing coins isn't difficult. All you need to do is to look up and search for the best product available.

The most important supplies for coin collecting

The condition of the coin is everything when it comes to the world of coin collecting. Within the realm of collecting coins it is the case that the coins by themselves are considered gold. This is the reason the reason why it is important to safeguard them from harm. The right equipment allows a collector to keep their integrity and value of the collection. Any slight sign of damage can reduce the worth of a piece of art significantly.

Here are a few items that are utilized to properly handle collections of coins:

Gloves

When handling coins, one must be cautious not scratching the surface of the coins. Gloves (preferably white) can prevent scratches as well as other types of scratching the surface of the coin. They must be made from either plastic or cotton.

Tweezers for coins

If you aren't comfortable wearing gloves, then you can try coins tweezers. They're not the usual tweezers because their tips are protected by plastic, which prevents the tweezers from scratching coins.

Magnifying glass

When looking at coins, you must be able to have a closer look at the coins. This is the place where the magnifying glass can be the most useful. Be cautious when using a magnifying device while looking at coins. There are magnifying glasses available these days that have stands attached to them. The stands allow the coin collector utilize both hands during scrutinizing coins to stay clear of any injuries.

Cleaning products

A mild soap along with a soft, high-integrity fiber cloth can be used to clean coins.

Mats

If you are cleaning or examining coins, be sure to use a soft, clean mat or cloth on the table you're working. A mishap with the coin could cause damage greatly and lower the value of the coin to almost zero. A mat or cloth can take the force of the drop and stop the coin from getting damaged.

Boards

You must be cautious when displaying your collection of coins. Coin boards are used by many people to showcase their collections of coins. The U.S., the map of the Us of America is quite popular among coin collectors to show the various quarters of each state.

Envelopes

For transporting coins, using coin envelopes is very practical. These envelopes permits a coin collector to securely transport his coins and also include some details about it inside or inside the envelope.

There are other equipment like containers, holders and and folders all of which contribute towards the care of coins and their state of preservation. The best kind of supply determines whether a particular valueless or unremarkable coin.

Designs of US Coins and Coin Collecting

At some point between 1838 and 1933, between 1838 and 1933, the Us introduced gold coinage to circulate. It was the Liberty Head bust was utilized as the symbol until 1907. The design was later altered to use that of the Indian Head and Saint Gaudens designs until 1933, in which it was the year that "Great Depression" was declared. This brought about the removal of the coins that makes it extremely difficult to come across any today.

The most sought-after coin around can be found in The 1933 Double Eagle. This was a gold coin made in the 1800's following the California gold rush. The coin was not permitted to be used in the 1930's. When this coin was auctioned off in 2002, it was sold for close to eight million dollars.

Since gold coins are extremely difficult to find, collectors tend to opt for other coins.

One type of collection you can think about is one that is comprised of coins that are damaged in the moment the coin was created. If you spot a coin with an incorrect spelling, incorrect date, off-center features or marks that are double-punched they are highly valuable. The occurrence of these errors could raise the value of a coin from $50 to $1000.

Coins issued only for a short period of time or circulated for a brief durations also are excellent collectibles.

A collection of coins will be the best when it's focused on a specific type of coin. The collector can select from pennies, nickels quarters, dimes and dollars.

Another method of collecting is to not consider the different types of coins and by focusing on a particular period of time. Coins are marked with various mint marks, and collecting the ones that were made in the same place could also be interesting. The most important thing for collectors is to maintain your collection till it's complete.

To get started, get a subscription to a coin publication like Coin World or Coinage Magazine to learn more about the kinds of coins you might be interested in collecting. A local or online coin shop can aid in the search for the coins that aren't located in your area or in other states.

The process of collecting coins will require a lot of time, months, or even years. The Us has produced an abundance of coins that it's difficult to keep on top of the number of coins. Once you have decided which coin(s) you wish to keep, the quest to complete your collection begins.

Chapter 13: Special Coin Sets

The U.S. has been, and continues to put premium versions of the coins that it mints every year in special holders such as cardboard or plastic to commemorate events and to provide people in general the coins that were minted in for the year. An excellent example of a unique set, which was released in the year 2019 is the set celebrating the 50th anniversary of Apollo 11. Apollo 11 mission.

It is the U.S. Mint web site is www.usmint.gov. I have included the address since it's easy to be confused by the words used by private companies which resembles those on the U.S. Mint site.

It is so numerous kinds of coins that the government offers each year that the best method to find out more about them is to go to the U.S. Mint website. Be aware that if you purchase a specific collection of coins, you should do so because they have an historical or sentimental significance for you, it is not an investment that is likely to increase in value over time. The majority of them do not increase in value, unless they have an uncommon coin or were made in small quantities. Be aware that some coins are offered every year as separate coins they are not part of the set.

To make this book more accessible, I'd like to concentrate on two sets since you'll find coins that belong to these sets when searching for half-dollars. The first is referred to as mint set, while the one that is called known as a proof set. You may be thinking the moment a coin is put into a holder that is specially designed such as of a plastic case, how will the coins be placed in the form of change?

For many who have such sets, the worth that the coin has is its"face" value, not their set value. They wish to use the money, but not even look at it or attempt to make it available for sale. They typically cut the case open and then spend the money. The change will end up in rolls in the future. Therefore, proof coins and mint coins are recycled. Be aware that certain sets contain silver coins inside however, some don't. Like we said earlier, weighing coins will aid in identifying them. The weight of silver is higher. A proof coin is an mirror-like surface on it.

Uncirculated or mint coins is shiny and beautiful however, it is not mirror-like.

An excellent way to know more about this subject is to study about what U.S. Mint states on their website, where they outline some of the sets that will be available in the year 2019:

"United Mint" annual coin sets are the foundational coins that make up the foundation of collecting.

The collection is available with stunning proofs and stunning uncirculated finishes these timeless favorites are great for any collection, and are a great way to begin a new collection and also make great presents for loved ones.

This year's annual sets comprises the 2019 , editions of United States Mint Proof Set, Silver Proof Set, Uncirculated Coin Set, and Limited Edition Silver Proof Set. Every set comes with all of the Native American $1 Coin, Kennedy half dollar Five America the Beautiful Quarters, Roosevelt dime, Jefferson nickel, and Lincoln penny. The coins are exquisitely designed with stunning, striking designs, these sets should be prominent within your collections!

As a bonus this year, if you purchase this year's proof, proof in silver and uncirculated coin sets , a free, version Lincoln penny featuring"W." West Point "W" mint mark will be sent to you in conjunction with each set. This is our way of saying

"thanks!" to our faithful customers. Get all three of the West Point special edition Lincoln pennies - only available during 2019!"

Did you observe it? The Mint mentions the proof set and silver proof set? uncirculated set, and limited edition sets of silver. This Mint advertisement doesn't mention all the sets or special coins being offered in 2019! Do you know how to keep track of this? When certain coins make through rolls and are altered in the course of time, how do you determine what kind of coin you're considering? Are they a half-dollar of a set from the mint Silver Proof Set, set that is uncirculated, limited edition set and so on?

The goal here isn't to be confusing. Most of the time there are only a handful of kinds of half dollars that you can find in these sets. One of them is an unproof half dollar that has no silver. A second is a proof half-dollar with silver. Both half dollars that are proof will have a mirror-like surface. Silver half dollars that are part of special sets that contain the proof as well as uncirculated coins will show occasionally. Take a look at the coin's weight, and you'll soon know the kind it is!

I'll provide the complete list of silver coins later.

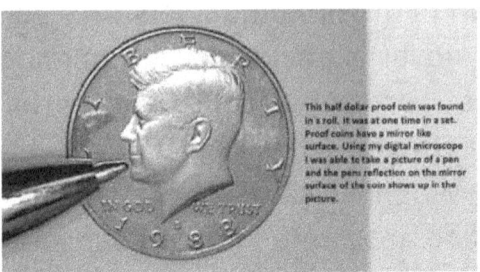

This half dollar proof coin was found in a roll. It was at one time in a set. Proof coins have a mirror like surface. Using my digital microscope I was able to take a picture of a pen and the pens reflection on the mirror surface of the coin shows up in the picture.

This image of a 2018 proof set from the San Francisco Mint has two silver coins in it: a dime and a half dollar. The 5 state quarters, the dollar, nickel, and penny are not silver.

However, the U.S. Mint also sold a 2018 proof set from the San Francisco Mint that looks exactly like this set, but has no silver coins in it.

The mirror like finish on the coins from both sets make it very hard to distinguish the silver and non silver half dollars from each other!

Half dollars in proof and half-dollars that have not been circulated are of no value after they are removed from their boxes, aside from their value in silver or as an error when they are containing it.

Half Dollar Errors and Rareties My heart never fails to skip when I am browsing through half-dollar rolls and find a stunning silver half-dollar. Bingo! If I can find a few in a single roll, I think I've hit the jackpot in the casino. When I discover amazing error coins worth much more than these silver coins I am reminded of the moment I was first introduced to half-dollar error through a close friend and how thankful I am to have this information. It was initially an effort to take a close look at every coin, and it was not enough effort. I was not able to find anything in the beginning. At first, I didn't realize the existence of an learning curve. After I had memorized all of the mistakes and became acquainted with how they appeared I was able to sort through coins at a fast speed and discover a lot of mistakes that are which are more valuable than the value of a silver coin.

What coin collectors are unaware of is the number of half-dollar error varieties you will find. The list is quite impressive. Although we'll concentrate specifically on Kennedy Half Dollar errors, some words about Walking Liberty, and Benjamin Halves are appropriate.

The reason I don't wish to place a great deal of weight on the two coins mentioned above is because there aren't any of them. If you do come across one, just take that year's year on the back of the coin as well as its mint mark, as well as the coin name and look it up. For instance, if you discover a 1958

"D" Benjamin Half Dollar Just go to Google and look up "1958 D Benjamin Half Dollar error" and then see what results come up. If you find something take a look at the coin and compare it with the errors listed online. Make this comparison for every coin you come across. I will include hyperlinks to the most serious Walking Liberty and Ben Franklin mistakes near the end of the book.

In the case of Kennedy Half Dollar, in regards to Kennedy Half Dollar, we must take a careful review of this book for each mistake, to help us find them. A useful reference chart will be included. A popular and widely well-known Kennedy Half Dollar error coins is the 1964 hair-accented half dollar. It was part of the initial series of proof coins created. As we mentioned previously, the coin was altered because the widow of President Kennedy thought that the hair's style was too striking and therefore needed to tone down. The amount of coins featuring this kind of hair is estimated to range from 40 to 120,000.

It's not easy to find these coins as it was part of an entire set however, why not search for these coins when you find 1964 halves (1964 without mintmark quarter dollars). Let's talk about what they look like. The hair of the type with accents has distinct and obvious strikes in comparison to the non accented kind. But to the untrained eye , it might be difficult to spot this. For us, there are other signs to look out for.

Alongside hairs, the particular error kind (not actually an error, it's just an additional die) also has other characteristics to look out for. Keep in mind the possibility that there exist many die varieties of 1964-dated coins. Each coin with an accent has the following features , in plus the hair anomaly however, not all of the features below will guarantee that you've got the right coin, since some of the features listed below are seen on coins without the hair that is accented. A coin with an accent must include the hair featureas well as all of the other features described below. When you have found these features, it is important to examine the hair, too.

On the reverse of the front of the "Accented Hair" coin the letter "I" in the word Liberty is not serif-like on the lower left side. The serif refers to the flat base the I sits on. On the reverse the rays on which the stars rest on are broken in contrast to solid rays in the version with no accents.

Another distinction can be seen in the reverse. The creator of the reverse on the coins has been identified as Frank Gasparro, as mentioned earlier. Initials "FG" underneath the right-hand leg of the eagle's head has no serifs on the type that is accented. The "G" is straight lines on it with no serif or top!

   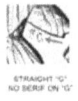

The accented hair coin shown above has all 4 features mentioned. If it has none of these features or only 3 of them and not the hair feature it is not an accented Kennedy Coin

Another coin worth being on the lookout for and one you are able to discover, and I have seen several of them, is the 1974 D Double Die Obverse. You'll become proficient in recognizing them after you've paid your taxes, and examine a large collection from 1974 D coins.

In the beginning, they can be difficult to identify. It is necessary to use a loupe. Pay attention to and study the "In God We Believe" motto found on the reverse of the 1974 "D" Coins. If it appears to be doubled, be sure to pay attention to the letters "R, U and S since these letters indicate an obvious double. A large portion of 1974 D coins you find are adorned with worn letters be sure to look at them carefully and take your time.

The same error (look at "R, U and S") is seen on a variety of Kennedy Half dollars, and new years that have this doubled appearance, are seen every day. But, the most famous errors are:

1971 to D 1973 – D

1972 1977 1972 1977

I would like to call the attention of two and possible more of the kind of error coins which are worth a tiny fortune. They've been found in circulation and are available in the form of change.

A strange error was made in 1971and was repeated in 1977. As you may know that in 1971, it was the year that U.S. Mint stopped using silver blanks to make half-dollar coins that circulated from 1971. Even though they made silver halves for sets that were special In 1970, they ended the use of the 40%.

silver halves made for general circulation.

Proof coins are made in the San Francisco Mint. If this mint determines that the planchets or blanks of coins do not meet the requirements to be used for Proofs, rather than throwing them away, it gives they to Denver Mint where they can be used to create coins that circulate. The blanks it sends are supposed to be copper-nickel clad and not silver. In 1971, and then again in 1977, they provided silver-claded blanks to Denver which was used to make half dollars composed from 40% silver, by error.

Although no one is sure the number of copies made however, they occasionally appear. In auctions, this mistake could fetch more than $10,000.00! If you have a 1971 D or 1977 D coin, it has an error, it could fetch more than $10,000.

This encapsulated 1971 D, 50C, 40% silver coin, was verified by NGC. It was graded at MS 61 or mint state 61 out of 70.

Here's a great example of how different Kennedy Half Dollars look when they contain 90% silver (coin on left) 40% silver (middle coin) and no silver (coin on right) Both silver coins have a distinct silver appearance, even under low light, while the non silver coin has a dull finish to it. This picture was taken using a newer cell phone. They take great pictures.

Silver appearance take a look at the silver appearance. Then weigh the silver appearance of the coin, weigh it. When it is 11.50 grams or more or less, it's 40% silver and you've struck the jackpot! Send it to evaluation to verify.

The 1964 coin on the left is 90% Silver – The coin on the right is 40 % Silver – You can see the slight difference but both have a silver appearance – Had this 1977 D coin in the middle been 40 % Silver it would look like the coin on the right

The coins that I've had amusement with the most since they are simple to findand possess high resale values, is those of the Kennedy Half Dollar "FG" coins. Like I said, Frank Gasparro designed the reverse of the Kennedy Half Dollar. The initials "FG" appear on the back of the coin under one of the legs on the left. Over the years, in both Denver Mint, and The Philadelphia Mint the letters "FG" are absent or missing in part.

It could be that there is no "FG" or no "F" and no "G" as well as any other combination in which some letter components are missing or present. The letter could also be weak letter or a strong letter. And one letter that is very incomplete and so on. I've found numerous types of letters that it's difficult to recall the entire list.

The years that this occurred are often found in these coinage: D There is no FG

1971 D . No F.

1972 D No FG

1973 D 1973 D - Aucune F (Also no G weak in F)

1977 D A - There was no F (Also no weak G with a weak F)

1980 D No FG

1982 P. No F.G. (Very fearful - just 55,000 minting)

1982 D No FG

1983 P No FG

1989 P . - Not a FG

1990 P. No FG

No "FG" on this Kennedy Half - The coin drawing on the right has the "FG" under the right leg.

On some coins the entire "FG" is missing
On others only part of the lettering is missing

The coin below has partial lettering: the "F" is gone-Part of the "G" remains

Remember that this type of error could be visible in the entire Kennedy Half!

A good example of a 1989 D Kennedy Half Dollar with a repunched mintmark – Magnification and patience are needed but coins like this, in good condition, can be worth a bundle!

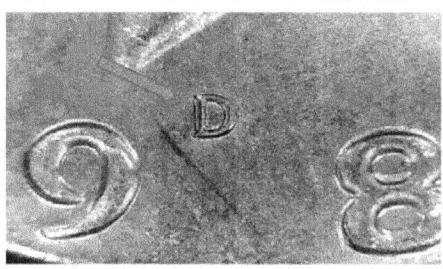

Another kind of error that has been seen on many instances of Kennedy Half Dollar years but is not often spotted in the form of a repunched mintmark. It takes a lot of

perseverance to locate these, and since the mintmark is tiny it requires an optical magnifier. The issue is with the mintmark. The mintmark is duplicated. It's surprising that this error has been discovered for several coins in the following years:

1964 to D1969 – S 1971 - 1972 - D 1984 D

1968-D 1969 D 1971 - D 1973 D 1989 D

Definition The term "repunched mintmark" is created when the letter-punch which is employed to insert the mintmark into the die creates two or more impressions offset.

The impressions usually are in a overlapping. A separate secondary mintmark is not common. The secondary mintmark is typically smaller and thinner than the standard mintmark.

This is because the top of the raised letters on the punch is more narrow that the bottom. Also, this raised letter of the punch taper vertically. The age of RPMs was ended in 1989 after they were replaced by the U. S. Mint began putting the mintmark onto the die master, instead of putting the mint mark into the die that was in use.

Here's a proof 1974 S half dollar found in change. Only a little over 2,000,000 were minted. It is not silver, but it has some of the outer mirror like finish peeling off the coin. This picture should be sent into some coin forums for evaluation. If it is a lamination error it might have some value.

There are many other types of errors you might encounter which at first glance might appear to be not worth taking care of. However, some of them are important and worth your time to find them.

Lamination issues can be discovered during the minting process , or following it.

Lamination errors are planchet mistakes that occur when the surface of a coin breaks and then flakes. Lamination issues can be present prior to or after strike. They're usually limited to coins made of solid alloy. The phrase "lamination mistake" is not grammatically correct since the metal actually is laminating.

I've witnessed a lot of mistakes in lamination as well as Kennedy Halves are no exception.

Other kinds of error you might encounter are clipped planchets, off-center and blank coins, rotated coins and many more. I'd like to briefly explain the most common errors to make sure you know that any unusual aspect of the coin you discover should be investigated further.

An investigation is required, since it could be a major error, as it could be a significant. I will give you great details on errors in coins towards the close in the text.

One of the simplest mistakes to identify, and worth the effort to identify is the coin rotation. The reverse rotates when compared with its front. If you're viewing the front of the Kennedy Half Dollar, and flip it over and back, it must be in alignment with the front and in the exact vertical location.

Rotated disalignment. In cases where struck pieces show a the misalignment of the dies, in particular during the coining process using dies that are mounted on round diestock, it is due to: (1) incorrect setup or human error of incompetence or misfortune; as well as (2) the dies are loose that could cause a chattering of the dies. This can eventually result in a struck piece that has rotated dies.

This is a mechanical fault regardless of how tightly the dies are seated into their chucks, a movement could cause them to loosen, making the dies spin.

Another kind you should be looking for is an unclipped planchet. It is simple to recognize. It appears like someone cut an area off of the coin's edge. This could mean a curly cut, straight cut, or any other kind of cut. There are various kinds of cut planchets that are clipped. The most well-known types are:

Clipped Planchet: Curved Clip

A curved clip is when the planchet strip isn't moved in the right direction after blanks have been punched out, which causes the blanking dies to cover holes that were previously punched out. This causes coins to have edges that have curved, which is and is referred to as a curved cut.

Clipped Planchet: Disc Clip

This clip is described as being a clip that is so small that it can be observed on the rim of the vessel or inside the

"shift" of metal around the edge, which doesn't affect the diameter of the coin by any means.

For instance there could be tiny dimples of metal missing from the rim, however the coin would be completely "round." If you have a coin that is clad, there will be a visible "shift" within the metal layers on the edge of the disc where the clip is located, however the coin will be totally round.

Chapter 14: Finding Rare and Collectible Coins

Coin collecting began as a pastime for the majority of people, however you might hear other people's stories (or you may have seen yourself) about people cashing in their old coins, which prompted many to embark on an avid collecting spree. If you're one of those who want to put money into coins, then here are some ways to begin your collection.

Coin Shops:

Many owners of shops are dealers with a lot of information on coins and also sell coins. Coin shops are an excellent source to discover and acquire more information on coins and collecting. The coin shops may be costly because they anticipate selling their collection for profit. With the right amount of knowledge and/or someone who knows a great amount about collecting coins at your side, you may find excellent deals on your old coins.

Coin Shows:

There are instances that your local mall will showcase a collection of dealers of coins. This lets you view the entire collection and enable you to purchase lots of coins at a reduced price because of the price competition. It is likely that you will also discover a variety of new coins that can be purchased and are suitable to your collection.

The coin shows are great not just for sellers and buyers, but also for coin enthusiasts who wish to view rare and difficult to locate coins.

Web Sites and Mail Orders:

There are many dealers across the world and many of their websites allow customers to customers purchase coins and pay via mail order or any payment method online like Paypal. It is recommended to do your own research on these businesses and be sure to read their terms carefully so that you are able to return your money if there is an issue with the currency you bought and/or received.

For every legitimate website there are numerous fake sites that are simply trying to steal your money. It is essential to get feedback from past customers prior to making any payments online. Also, remember not to reveal any pin or password.

Flea Markets:

It's a bit of a surprise to discover rare coins in an auction, but strange things have occurred. They have different views about price, because of their lack of understanding of the way a coin should be priced. It is common to find coins that are priced too high however if you're fortunate, you may come across an unusual coin in those piles of coins which can be worthwhile to look at it.

Flea market sellers are typically trying to sell their items quickly and are likely to offer you discounts when you purchase their products in the bulk. Consider buying other items and then get coins to your purchase as a bonus.

Auctions:

If you're seeking to invest in rare coins, the best option is an auction. Auctions are the only way that you can find individuals selling their most sought-after and expensive coins. Many auctions happen online at once , and many sellers are searching for the most bidders. Beware and be aware that a lot of the sellers are frauds and won't make the money you pay a profit. It is important to find out more about these coins before trying to purchase one through an auction site.

Additional Coin Collectors

Coin collectors typically have duplicate coins they would like to sell at a lower price than its value. The problem is that it's hard to locate a coin collector who has the same type of coins as you. The most effective places to search are forums, online communities, and (in the event that you already have an existing one) locally-based groups.

Coin collectors from other countries are the best people to talk to when you're looking to begin your personal collection. They can give you advice or discounts, and some could even offer you a few their coins to help you start your collection.

Like any other investment where the value fluctuates. They may decrease in value and/or increase in value at any moment. The most effective way to earn money when collecting coins is to keep current with the latest information and prices for the coin. This will not only aid you to avoid being misled by dealers, but also by understanding how to value coins without having an inventory of prices.

Chapter 15: Selling your Coin Collection

If you began your coin collection to enjoy a hobby or to invest in eventually, you will reach the time that you look into selling the coins that you've collected. You may need to do this due to a financial requirement or to aid a family member or friend. It is certain that you are not selling them because you've had enough of them or have lost interest. As with all commodities you're expecting an acceptable value to be offered for them, and you anticipate some sort of profit through the transaction, regardless of how small. The goal is to receive the highest amount of money from your coins as swiftly and easily as is possible.

There are a variety of options available in auctioning off your items. You could opt for an auction for the public. The majority of auction houses require a minimum consignment amount. If your collection is less than this amount, they'll not take your collection. The next step is to find a different dealer who accepts lower worth coins and will auction them off for you fast.

Another method of selling your collection is to have an individual sale. It is the most efficient method but also the most risky and lengthy. It is necessary to approach multiple vendors and propose your coins up for auction. It is possible that you will not find an individual who can offer an acceptable price for them. You could also place an advertisement in the local paper however some of the offers that you receive through these could be questionable in nature. It could be too late to accept an offer from a con artist who is trying to extort money from those who are similar to you.

Another option to decide to send your coins to an individual dealer. You must only do this if you know the details about the background of the dealer. Find out if the dealer will accept the coins in exchange for the amount of a certain amount, over which he/she could charge the markup. The majority of dealers will agree as they don't have any capital investment since the markup will be a guaranteed profits.

In this article we will consider the other option, which is personal sale.

The first thing to determine is the specifics of what's in your collection and what they're worth to yourself as well as the dealer and buyers. You must know what you'll be selling so you should conduct some research. The first step to do is create an inventory of your collection. You must identify every coin to know what each one is worth and what the entire collection is worth. You might already know, particularly if you've bought each of them.

You may even believe that, based on your calculation of the amount you paid when you bought the coins, plus a markup you'd make some substantial profits, don't you think? Additionally, if read about the value of coins, you'd recognize that a specific coin in your collection could be worth this amount. Well, it depends. Be aware that the amount you paid for your coins as well as the prices in those magazines are retail prices , and not what a dealer might be willing to pay. A lot of the value is contingent on the condition of the collection. It is necessary to have them examined for any damages. The bottom line isthat you won't get what you want and it could be lower.

You could also consult one of the references listed above The "Official Red Book: A Guide Book of United States Coins." It will provide you with an estimate of the approximate the value of your coins.

You must now locate a dealer who will assess your coins accurately. Research and study the background of any dealers you are considering. You can locate them on the official website of the Professional Numismatic Guild (PNG). It is important to know that dealers are trustworthy members who are in good standing with the American Numismatic Association (ANA) or any other recognized numismatic association. You might have to learn through trial and error however, now you need to be sure that the person you select is trustworthy and will tell you what the actual value of your coins is.

Once you've decided on a dealer, take arrangements to contact the dealer. This can be done via phone or email, If you have one. If you call them, you must identify yourself. let them know that you plan selling your collections, and present them with the inventory lists you made earlier. If you're lucky you might be able to get the dealer to accept your collection. If not, and the dealer isn't attracted by your collections since it's not a high-end one and they won't be able to make any profit, you should go to the next dealer on your list.

The dealer who takes your collection will offer an offer that may sound quite disconcerting to the buyer. It is likely that the dealer won't offer the price you expected instead, they will offer the wholesale price that is considerably less that the price retail. Keep in mind your original price were imagining in your mind was what you would pay for the coins at retail, not the price you're willing be willing to pay in exchange for coins.

The price the dealer gives you is the amount the dealer will offer to ensure that they is able to make a profit once your collection is auctioned off. Additionally the dealer reserves the right to alter the price based on the state of your coins. The dealer might not be in agreement with the condition of the coins that you thought of and when the dealer's offer is less you can expect a significant reduction in the price. If, for some reason or another, you can't come to a deal that is acceptable to you both then go to the next dealer on your list.

In your look for the right dealer, you might be interested in selling some of the items you have to auction houses. If your collection is in line with the criteria of the auction house, you may be able to negotiate an increase in price. However,

Make sure you are aware of the costs involved and then do some calculations. It is possible that you will win in this particular case.

In the event that an offer that is acceptable for you has been accepted and you've made the decision to sell, you may or invite the buyer to your home or, in the case that the buyer is far away, in a different city, state, or even state you could decide to send your collection by the mail. It is a risk however there are steps you can follow to ensure your coins are delivered safely to their doorsteps.

Be sure to package carefully, taking care to avoid any loose coins that might bounce around in the packaging and be advertised as valuable coins. Include a list of items so that the purchaser can easily verify the items upon arrival. This is why USPS

Priority Mail is a secure method to send the items. Choose the most affordable shipping option for you. Make sure that the coins are insured to ensure your security and include an additional cost to confirm delivery.

Conclusion

When you first opened the book you may be unaware about what coin collecting was and what the most effective techniques are for people who wish to become "professional coin collectors."

In this moment you're likely to find that you've already learned a great deal beginning with the various types of coins , before moving to the places you can buy your coins as well as where you are able to sell them.

You may feel that you're overwhelmed with details, and that's totally normal. Coin collecting isn't an entirely new thing in any way. However, it certainly has an arduous learning curve, particularly when it comes to the particulars of each type of coin, how you can find them and how to get the most of them as the seller.

Experience and time will have an impact on you, I assure you. Don't be discouraged and don't rush and avoid making decisions that you regret later. Keep to the advice we've discussed in this book and you'll in the near future be the proud proprietor of a newbie coin collection.

I am aware that this book doesn't tell you all the information there is on coin collections. However, I'm worried that it would have required the entire library to complete the task but even then, I would have missed out quite a bit of information.

In closing, as a tip If there's something I've personally found beneficial in my journey to becoming a coin-collector it was getting to know other like-minded individuals. I cannot stress this enough If there's anything I strongly suggest you to try from now from now, it's joining clubs to begin learning! There's gold in these clubs!

I wish you best of luck on your journey. You may be in the beginning right now but I'm here to tell you that the path ahead is only paved with silver, gold as well as... Jingles!

Thank you for taking the time to start your journey with me and the guidance I provided you with here!

www.ingramcontent.com/pod-product-compliance
Lightning Source LLC
Chambersburg PA
CBHW071836080526
44589CB00012B/1013